C000156349

THE HAUNTED TOUR
OF
BRITAIN

MERSEYSIDE

Happy Haunting

The Haunted Tour of Britain

of

Britain

Merseyside

By Richard Felix

FELIX FILMS

First published in Great Britain in 2007 by
Felix Films Ltd
Derbyshire

ISBN 978-0-9557535-0-3

Printed and bound by Biddles Ltd, Hardwick Industrial Estate,
King's Lynn, Norfolk.

CONTENTS

ACKNOWLEDGEMENTS

The production of this book would never have been possible without the knowledge and expertise of:

Julia Felix

Derek Acorah

Gwen Acorah

Steve Parsons

Daniel Mason

and staff at Croxteth Hall

FOREWORD

I was delighted when I learned that Richard Felix was about to publish a book concentrating on the ghosts of Merseyside and more than honoured when he asked whether I would add a word or two in the form of this foreword.

I first met Richard some six years ago during the filming of a paranormal programme upon which we were both working. The place was Derby Gaol. Upon meeting him, I was immediately taken by Richard's incredible enthusiasm as he related the history of the location and his obvious love of his home town of Derby.

As I was to find out over the ensuing years, Richard's knowledge of the history of our country and beyond is boundless. His manner of delivering the facts is riveting. I have spent many hours with Richard during paranormal investigations in some very strange and dark places waiting for "something to happen". During those times he has fascinated me with some of his stories of days gone by. I am sure that within the pages of this, Richard's latest book, you will be equally enthralled.

I can think of no one better to tell the story of some of the ghostly goings on in the Merseyside area in general and my beloved home town of Liverpool in particular than Richard Felix, Ghost Historian Extraordinaire!

DEREK ACORAH

PREFACE

In 1992 Richard Felix decided that his hometown of Derby desperately needed a Heritage Centre as a catalyst for him to tell the history of his city, not only to its residents but also to the whole world. Little did he realise what a far-reaching effect the opening of this centre would have and that it would lead to the origins of the now world famous Derby Ghost Walks, that have attracted people from all over the world, which has now established Derby as 'The Ghost Capital of England'.

The walks not only tell the ghost stories of the city but also delve into the fascinating history behind them. Richard is a great believer that ghosts and history go together.

The ghost walks have evolved over the last fourteen years and now offer the public two different experiences. The City Centre Ghost Walk, starting from The Old Bell in Sadlergate, tells the infamous story of PC Moss, the only police officer in Derbyshire to be murdered in the line of duty. After hearing this story it is time for a well earned drink in The Old Tiger Inn before descending into the Guildhall Tunnels - where you might get the fright of your life. The walk continues around the city centre visiting various haunted sites including The Jorrocks Pub, final resting place of a screaming skull. The tour finishes back at the Old Bell with a visit to the attic room haunted by the ghost of a serving maid. The evening concludes with a candle-lit supper in the Old Tudor Bar.

With the success of The City Centre Ghost Walk, Richard discovered another building which was to add to the ghostly stories and tell the tales of crime and punishment in Derby. This was the Derby Gaol, located in the basement of 50/51 Friar Gate. This building was erected in 1756 and was the second of three county gaols in Derby. It remained a place of incarceration and execution until 1840. Richard set about restoring it to its original structure with his usual enthusiasm and expertise.

During the renovation the original graffiti was discovered on the cell doors. These were the carvings of prisoners scratching their initials on them the day before they were hanged. The public are now able to visit the gaol and wander around the cells seeing the condemned cell and the etchings for themselves. The Hangsman Walk was born starting from the Derby Gaol telling the stories of murders, executions and ghostly occurrences. The visitor starts with a brief tour of the Gaol before heading down Agard Street, to hear of the harrowing murder of Eliza Morrow in 1862. Continuing down Friar Gate for the first haunted pub stop, Seymours, there is a picture of the Victorian lady who haunts the pub to this day. The walk continues into the cellars of the Old Friary before returning to the Gaol for supper and then unlike so many others, the visitor will be allowed to return home after making sure that no one follows them.

The fame of these walks and Derby Gaol spread worldwide and as a result Richard came to the notice of the hugely popular Living TV programme 'Most Haunted'. The team came along and carried out interviews, paranormal investigations with the latest hi-tech ghost hunting equipment. On returning to the editing studios they could not decide which part of Richard's interview to edit - as a result Richard was appointed as the resident paranormal historian on the programme - and the rest is most haunted history!

Derby Gaol has now become a major tourist attraction and one of the 'must do' haunted locations in this country. Offering not only ghost walks but night vigils, using the latest equipment and offering the services of a spiritualist medium.

Richard realised how the public are excited about ghost hunting and the history connected to buildings and set about the enormous and time-consuming task of creating the Ghost Tour Of Great Britain. For this purpose he needed a camera man to aid the completion of this tour and this resulted in him joining with Steve Lilley for the production of books and DVD's called 'The Ghost Tour Of Great Britain.' They have now visited over 40 counties throughout England, Scotland and Wales. In September 2005 Richard's youngest son William set up his own production company called 'Felix Films Ltd' which will endeavour to complete Richard's tour of Haunted Britain.

14

PART ONE
What is a Ghost?

I have been haunted by ghosts all my life, I am not a medium, I am not a psychic, I do not see dead people but I am frightened of ghosts. After years of study and countless fascinating experiences, I now consider myself an expert in the paranormal. I was a ghost virgin until the age of 27.

As a child the very thought of spirits, ghouls and skeletons filled me with fear and dread. I was petrified of ghosts, and to a certain extent, I am still to this day. When I was no more than four I was locked in a huge rabbit hutch in a garage by so called older friends and told that the Green Ghost was going to get me. Experiences such as this only served to fuel an already vivid imagination and as a child I would refuse to stay alone in any building, never venture upstairs without someone's hand to hold and certainly never walk past a churchyard alone. I spent most nights as a youngster with the light on, beneath my bedclothes with my fingers firmly crossed, waiting for that demonic being to appear at the foot of my bed, pull back my bedclothes and reveal its hideous face. Thank God this never happened and it never will but perhaps my way of facing up to my fears was to discover all I possibly could about ghosts and why they haunt.

In 1992 I started to conduct ghost walks around the city of Derby. Fifteen years later, over 200,000 people have been on a ghost tour of my home city. Derby's location in the centre of the country has underlined its importance for nearly 2000 years and contributed to its prosperity. It has always been the crossroads of history. Some people went on to greater things, others turned back, some stayed, some died in battle, others were imprisoned or executed.

For these and many other reasons Derby has become 'The Ghost Capital of England, The Dead Centre'.

However, every region in Great Britain has its own folklore, legends and ghost stories and in recognition of this I embarked on The Ghost Tour of Great Britain with a film crew. In the last four years we have visited 40 counties looking for ghosts, talking to people who have witnessed ghosts and visiting haunted places. My experiences as an expert on the popular TV programme 'Most Haunted' have widened my horizons still further and put me in direct contact with some of the scariest places in this country. Even today I am still learning and remain grateful to the folklorists and parapsychologists who continually surprise me with their thoughts and theories.

My quest in life is to prove beyond all doubt that there is life after death and that the dead do return.

Most parapsychologists and scientists don't believe in life after death and put most paranormal activity down to the influence of the living, not the dead. They believe most people are mistaken, overtired, drunk, displaying vivid imagination or are just making it up. They attribute many unexplained events to ESP (Extra Sensory Perception) i.e. the powers of living individuals who have the ability to move items with their minds. At least ESP and the idea of telepathic understanding between living creatures is a more comfortable theory to swallow than the spectre of the dead returning or being trapped on this earth as punishment for terrible crimes through the trauma, fear or pain of an unexpected death.

The idea of sharing our world - sometimes our own homes or places of work with the spirits of dead people is very disturbing, but I have interviewed thousands of ordinary, sane, sober individuals with no axe to grind, who swear they have encountered a ghost. For now please make a note of the Richard Felix rules for ghost hunting. First and foremost you need to be enthusiastic. Second, you need to be a detective and third you need to be sceptical. You have to research and explore all avenues when you look into a ghosts' history and try to get to the bottom of the reason for the haunting.

For most people that would be enough. However, I passionately believe the ultimate aim of the real ghost hunter is to ask: "How can I help"? If you are looking for nothing more than the cheap thrill of a scary experience go and watch a horror movie or go to a theme park. I believe that there is a responsibility attached to ghost hunting. If an animal lover tracks down a caged gorilla, does he simply take a photograph of the unfortunate monkey and walk away? No he does not, that is not enough - the final act has to be the release of the tormented creature from its "imprisonment, pain and anguish". It is therefore important to understand that ghosts- whether the product of the living or the dead - haunt places for different reasons. Some are happy so let them stay but some wish to be released. Their appearance before you, their taps and raps, their moans and groans are all a cry for help from beyond the grave.

So for their sake, in fact for every ones sake, we should be helping them to find release from their earthly torment.

Although I believe in ghosts, I have seen two, heard one and travelled with one. I am still the world's biggest sceptic. I believe that eight out of ten ghostly occurrences can be explained, it's the other two that you have got to be worried about. (The wind did blow the door shut, you just didn't notice that the window was open. The dark shadow leaving your bedroom was in fact your Dad looking for a pair of socks in your drawer).

I have to tell you that much of what folks see, hear and believe to be supernatural is nothing more than a recording. It is not an intelligence and is not self aware. It cannot communicate or interact with you. It is nothing more than a recording. It is no more exciting or frightening than pressing the replay button of a DVD player. Instead of being recorded onto a shiny disc or a piece of plastic tape, it is recorded into the fabric of the building. It's called the STONE TAPE THEORY. Stone buildings such as castles and old halls can hold recordings of tragic and traumatic events. Sandstone especially is an ideal medium because it contains silica, iron oxide and water which is found in recording tapes, and it is my belief that the energy emanates from the stone when atmospheric conditions are right or a person is for want of a better word 'tuned in'.

I believe we all have a pre-ordained moment when we should die. Sometimes by accident this is brought forward due to battles, car or plane accidents, murders, suicides or executions. In fact your time had not come and the energy used by the body in resisting death can be so immense, the electrical impulses given off by the brain moments before death can be so great, that the actual event just before death takes place can be recorded into the bricks, mortar, woodwork and plaster of a building, also into the damp soil on battlefields.

This is why you see the apparition as it was just before death, fully clothed, thank goodness but how can you see the ghost of someone's clothes, sword, bagpipes or carriage. They don't have souls or spirits. The person has to be alive to make the recording. I have recently learnt that the brain continues to emit electro magnetic signals for up to twenty seven hours after death. What about that then?

Seeing an apparition should be no more frightening than watching John Wayne in an old cowboy film. It is only a recording that you see on the screen. He cannot interact with you i.e. 'pop out' of the screen and ask you to put the kettle on. He is not an intelligence, he is just a recording on a piece of plastic tape. In the same way as you play your favourite film over and over again, the quality deteriorates through use. This results in a lady originally wearing a red dress in the 17th Century, fading to pink in the 18th Century, to grey in the 19th Century and finally a wispy grey haze in the 20th Century before fading away completely.

If I was to take you back in time to 1650 and then try to explain how I had been able to record onto a strip of brown plastic video tape an event which had happened months ago (perhaps some of the people at the event may have died) put it into a slot and show you the event again and again on a glass screen, I would have been taken out and hanged, or burnt at the stake as a witch! Today we accept it as the norm; we wouldn't run away screaming "I've seen a ghost". What I'm saying is it possible that with enough energy you can record onto other fabrics as well as CD's, DVD's, photographic paper, video tape, mini discs and magnetic cassettes. In other words, the fabric of a building can also hold a recording.

People frequently report seeing ghosts walk through walls, appearing to be either headless or legless. That is probably because the building has changed since the recording was made. The doorway has been bricked up, plastered and wallpapered. The ceiling or the floor may be lower or higher, the stairs may no longer be there.

Probably the most famous ghost story in the world will explain what I mean. It was the 1950's, young Harry Martindale was a heating engineer in York. He was digging a hole in the cellar of Treasurer's House, a very haunted building in the centre of York. He was alone when he heard a trumpet blast. The mind can't cope with "I've just heard a Roman trumpet". He just put it down to car hooters or a transistor radio until twenty Roman soldiers came through the cellar wall. They appeared to be very small. In fact, they were legless (without legs, not drunk). Harry was terrified, he hid behind some rubbish in the cellar and watched them pass by. They did not respond to him and did not look at him. When they reached a trench he could see their legs. They continued through the cellar and passed through the opposite wall. Harry ran and told his mates who laughed at him, as did many people who heard his rather incredible story. Until one day they did an archeological dig underneath Treasurer's House. There fifteen inches below the cellar floor they found an old Roman road on the exact route that Harry had seen his ghostly soldiers. The new cellar floor being fifteen inches higher than the original Roman road.

No one really understands the immense power of the human mind and how it can react in times of stress, trauma and emotional upset. How many times have you heard stories of super human acts such as a frail woman lifting a car off her trapped child? We call it superhuman strength, but is it? We just do not understand it.

I believe that in the not too distant future we will find a way to unleash recordings of traumatic historical events that lie deeply encapsulated in the fabric of a building.

Although what I have just referred to is only a recording, there are entities, souls and spirits that have not moved on. In death as in life they are an intelligence and have chosen to stay rather than move on. There are various reasons for this. They do not know they are dead, they love the place, house, workplace, person or vehicle and do not want to leave or they are too frightened to move on. The church has a great deal to answer for. It has ruled by fear for nearly two thousand years. Why should he be referred to as a "God fearing man"? Why should we fear God? This is what we have been taught since the beginning of Christianity. The Ten Commandments, Judgment Day, the Seven Deadly Sins, Hell Fire and Damnation have all led to people being afraid of breaking any of these beliefs. If they did break these rules they would be destined for hell fire! So would you risk trying it on at the 'Pearly Gates' to be told "go straight to hell". I know what I would do, I would stay here.

Are poltergeists dead or are they living?

Many poltergeist cases over the centuries have centred on pre-pubescent children especially girls. Examples of this are:- The Schiel case in Germany in the 1580's, the North Aston case 1590's, Epworth Rectory 1716, Cock Lane 1760's, Bell Witch 1817, the Stans case Switzerland 1860 and the Enfield case 1970's.

Most of these famous cases involved taps, raps and movement of objects. In modern times poltergeists have discovered that there is

Objects flying around a sleeping child.

fun to be had with electric light bulbs, phones and computers.

It is possible that a living human not a spirit may be responsible for the poltergeist activity. The term widely used is RSPK (Recurrent Spontaneous Psycho Kinesis).

In a nutshell this means mind waves controlling matter, emanating from someone at or near the outbreak. In other words they are the poltergeist themselves, they are the energy creating the chaos, they are the unwitting cause of the things that happen around them and have no conscious control over them.

The phenomena caused is in some way or other the outcome of a highly emotional state or conflict which has been denied conscious expression or the relief it brings.

In some way emotional tension, anxiety, aggressive urges or suppressed sexual excitement generate the energies which exhibit themselves in what we refer to as poltergeist activity.

A very interesting case took place in 1975 when a new shopping centre opened in Derby. Within days of opening alleged poltergeist activity was reported from various shops. Some of the phenomena were only experienced at weekends when a large percentage of staff were part time Saturday kids. A great deal of joking took place at first but fear soon started to spread. The information was partly suppressed for fear of an adverse effect on sales within certain chain stores.

It was around this time that the city council decided that professional help was needed. All staff were advised to keep a record of events and report any strange occurrences to the council. The outbreak became so serious that exorcisms were carried out in the basements of some shops and Derby Borough Council issued a pamphlet to the shop workers entitled 'Your poltergeist and how to deal with it'.

The following is an excerpt:

A: Its' History

1. *Poltergeists are quite common and have been recorded for many hundreds of years.*

2. *At present cases are being researched and documented in the United States where the work of Dr Rhine of Duke University, and of Roll and the Morrises in England is noteworthy.*

3. *Many people down the ages and many people today, have and are suffering from pranks of their poltergeist.*

B: Its Nature

4. It is not an illusion and can produce physical effects which can be weighed, measured and recorded: i.e. it can move things and it can produce noises…

5. It is attached to and part of the mind of an owner or group of owners…

6. The poltergeist feeds on fear, although it is harmless both to soul and body and is, in its own way, a relief to the suffering mind.

7 Its owner has no control over it and is unaware of his or her ownership.

C: How to deal with it.

8. Once the pressures which have produced it are understood, the Poltergeist will fade out.

9 Where premises have been affected; a ritual blessing will greatly help to calm the atmosphere of strain and fear.

Many members of staff from several shops experiencing the phenomena did make themselves familiar with the pamphlet but it still continued. More exorcisms took place but the poltergeist activity continued for some time afterwards.

Psychotherapy was used on some staff members with better results, which proves in some cases that it can banish poltergeist activity. If it is right to look to the person concerned for the source of the phenomena, then we may be able to discover why it suddenly ceases. Perhaps some change in their emotional or mental state could mean he or she is no longer producing the extra quantities of energy and therefore the rappings, levitations and stone throwing will naturally stop.

In any event, the mind over matter theory is not endorsed by all investigators. Some believe that only a proportion of poltergeists can be explained in this way and the reason that the activity stops is because the malevolent spirit gets fed up, packs its bags and goes 'home'!

Crisis Apparitions

Remember we are nothing but energy. Each one of us emits 2 kilo-watts of electricity each day. We are the best computer ever invented. The more machines we invent the lazier we become. Thousands of years ago primitive man was able to communicate by telepathy, we have now invented mobile phones, but we are still capable of communicating with our mind. The number of times I say to my wife, "get off my wave length, I was going to say that or I was going to phone you". Many stories abound from the first and second world war of soldiers appearing before their mothers or wives and days later a telegram comes to tell them they have been killed in action. These are examples of some form of telepathic link between people who love each other. Sometimes the apparition or ghost as it is called doesn't die. There are various cases reported of ghosts of living people, whose appearance can cause a loved one to summon help, thus stopping a tragedy. Most of us at some time or other get a feeling that makes us visit a friend or loved one who is very ill and we often arrive just in time to say goodbye.

Phantasm

These are ghosts of living people. When the society for psychical research did a survey in 1888 they discovered that many people were able to put a name to the ghosts that they had seen. In fact these apparitions were in no danger and were still alive. We have an amazing ability through our energy to project our image to a place that we would rather be or a place that we love.

There is an amazing account of a baker who retired after many years in the same bakery. After a few weeks his ghost was reported in the bakery that he had once owned. The new owners, believing that he had died, contacted the family only to be told he was alive and well. He had always got up at four o'clock in the morning to start baking and after retirement still got up at the same time. He would go downstairs, make a cup of tea and sit by his gas fire thinking of the work that he use to do in the bakery and somehow through his own energy projected his image back to the place where he spent so many years of his life.

So you want to be a Ghosthunter?

The first thing any Ghost Hunter needs to consider is what is normal, rather than what is paranormal. Most ghostly occurrences can be explained. What does paranormal mean?… It means running alongside the normal. What does supernatural mean?… What we do not understand, we fear. This fear can add to our conception of what we see, enhancing our emotions and reactions. If there is an entity within the building, it can also feed on our emotional fears. When and if something does happen, start ticking off the normal boxes first and if there are any boxes left at the end "whoopee"! you may have found or seen a ghost. The majority of scientific discoveries have been made by amateurs, so there is a high possibility that a ghost could be recorded beyond all doubt by an amateur group of paranormal investigators with the most basic of equipment. This basic equipment consists of candles, torch, tape recorder, thermometer and dictaphone. However, the biggest and most important thing for any ghost investigator to have is patience. Ghosts or paranormal activity does not happen when you want it to. Ghosts do not 'jump through hoops' or perform for audiences. Most ghostly activity occurs when most people are not really expecting anything to happen but they have been emotionally open and receptive to their surroundings for some reason…trauma, excitement, fear and shock. Candles are simple but very effective as they are very sensitive to

Richard with his dowsing crystal

any slight draft or movement and always create a soft light. This light given off from a candle can be either relaxing or ghostly depending on the mood of the people in the room and how active ones imagination is. Dictaphones and tape recorders are useful but do not need to be left recording for hours. They can be far more effective if the use of them is controlled and they are used to record answers to questions, such as "Is there anyone there"? Sitting listening to tape recordings for hours is often soul destroying and impractical, two minutes is quite enough.

Being a paranormal historian I tend to favour the old fashioned techniques of ghost hunting which involves the use of dowsing rods, crystals, tilting tables and even ouija boards (UNDER STRICT SUPERVISION AND ADULT CONTROL). These traditional methods can often give you answers but remember it can only be very basic, i.e. yes or no. The problem I have is whether the message is coming from a spirit which answers our questions, or whether the message is coming from our subconscious… we are without knowing influencing the movement and response of these things. The ouija board can tell us much more than just yes and no. It frequently responds with complete words and even sentences. Do not get despondent if you only get "Gobbledygook" because many years ago the vast majority of people could not read or write and their alphabet was very different to the one we use today.

The question I am frequently asked is "Are ouija boards dangerous"? I suggest that they are only used by people that know what they are doing and do not leave anyone open to any distress or interference from beyond. I do not think there is any difference standing in a circle holding hands asking "Is anybody there"? or sitting around a table asking the same question. If someone is evil in life there is every possibility that they could be evil in death. Using the universal law of 'likes attract', if there is an evil person around the table or in the circle they could attract their own kind. SO FOR THIS REASON I WOULD STRESS THAT YOU DO NOT TRY THIS AT HOME!

Just remember all the scientific equipment being used is only based on us, our minds and brains. We are the best computer ever created and are therefore the best ghost detector.

So at the end of the day all of this equipment can only justify to others that the temperature really has dropped. When carrying out paranormal investigations, one of the most common changes in the atmosphere that people experience is a chill or draft. This can be easily detected by a simple thermometer but even more so by a laser thermometer that will tell you exactly where a drop in temperature occurs. Do remember the laser thermometer will only record the temperature where the tip of the beam makes contact, which is usually the wall or floor. To record the temperature where the apparition appeared, you need a probe thermometer which can be 'dangled' exactly where the activity has taken place.

The trusty EMF meter used by most ghost hunters and waved around on most TV ghost hunting programmes, is not a ghost detector. As far as I know ghosts do not emit an electromagnetic signal. You so often see on TV a medium saying "the ghost is

The EMF meter

standing over there in the corner" and the investigator walks over to the ghost waving his EMF meter around - rubbish! What you should be doing is waving the EMF meter around the head of the person who is seeing the ghost to check if there is a fluctuation in EMF caused by a badly earthed wire near to them. This can cause a change in the frequency of their brain which could cause them to see a ghost.

When visiting a haunted location I try to interview as many people as possible who are connected with the building. You need to be inquisitive and methodical like a police detective and you also need a confident interviewing technique but one that puts people at their ease. Let them do the talking and record the conversations. However, always make sure you have the person's permission to record what they say. The most credible witnesses are those who live

Richard interviewing Harry Martindale in the cellars of Treasurer's House, York.

or work in the building as they know the building like 'the back of their hand'. They know the familiar and characteristic sites and sounds of the building. You should give more credence to the person who tells you what they have seen, without giving a reason for the ghost i.e. I was told this place was once a monastery and therefore the ghost must be a monk. Beware of linking a ghost of a famous person with the building just because they had an association with it i.e. they lived or worked there. An example of this is Anne Boleyn is said to haunt the area around the scaffold in the Tower of London.

"How do you know it's Anne Boleyn?

Because she is wearing a Tudor dress.

All women wore Tudor dresses in Tudor times".

Anne's execution, although traumatic, was not as grisly as

other executions that took place there. If anyone should haunt that area, it should be the ghost of seventy seven year old Margaret Pole. This poor lady ran away from the execution block and the executioner chased her around the scaffold wielding his axe until he eventually succeeded in hacking her to death.

Most folks that see a ghost are not frightened when they see them. The mind has an amazing tendency to rationalize what it has seen. It cannot cope with the idea that "I have just seen a ghost"! It is only when it vaporizes or disappears through the wall, the person realises that they really have seen a ghost… that is when reality and shock can set in. Once you have seen a ghost you have to become your own detective just as I did when I saw a ghost in Derby Gaol at three twenty on a Friday afternoon. It was a grey hazy figure, neither male or female, it was in full vision and not out the corner of my eye. The apparition lasted for at least six seconds and I sensed it as well as seeing it. Since this ghostly experience I have explored all eventualities to prove that it was not steam from the dishwasher, smoke from the fire or sunlight through the window, no EMF recording and no infra sound. After eliminating all possibilities I can only come to one conclusion… "I SAW A GHOST"!

If you use a medium during your investigation, either in a séance or vigil, do not fall into the trap that most TV programmes fall into of making the programme into 'let's test the medium'. Take them to the location yourself, do not tell them where your going and make sure someone stays with them. If you have two mediums, try and keep them apart and interview them separately. If they have the same information and emotions in the same areas then you could well be onto something. I believe that the vast majority of mediums and psychics do have an ability. It is a gift, an extension of our five senses rather than a sixth. In the same way as we are all capable of playing the piano but few of us will never become a concert pianist. Some people can even play the piano without having the ability to read music. I cannot play the piano so they cannot but they can prove it by playing me a tune whereas the medium cannot show us the ghost. I believe in ghosts and the supernatural. Therefore I have to believe in mediums. Whether they are communicating with our dead relatives or just have an ability to read our minds. Do they retrieve the memories of our dead loved ones in exactly the same way as the police can retrieve erased data from a computer? Do remember eight out of ten ghostly occurrences can be explained... it's the other two you have to worry about.

Happy Hauntings!

PART TWO

The Haunted Tour of Britain

of

Britain

Merseyside

INTRODUCTION

Merseyside is located in the North – West of England and is named after the River Mersey. The county came into existence when it was created in 1974 by the local government act of 1972.

Merseyside is made up of a number of different boroughs which are Liverpool, Knowsley, St Helen's, Sefton, and the Wirral. The county is divided into two parts by the estuary of the river but they are linked by the Mersey railway tunnel and the famous Mersey ferry. The county has a population of over one and a half million and covers an area of two hundred and fifty two square miles.

The main city of Merseyside is Liverpool and is unusual because it has two cathedrals --- The Roman Catholic Cathedral and an Anglican Cathedral. In 1190 the city was known as 'Liuerpul', which means a pool with muddy water. In 1207 Liverpool was granted borough status by King John. Liverpool today has become one of the 'must places' to visit on everyone's tourist list because of its history, architecture and its contribution to music and its ghosts. This city is very much a city of the 21st century and the John Lennon Airport (named after one of the famous Beatles) welcomes visitors from all over the world.

Liverpool has become famous for two things which are both close to everyone's heart --- music and football. One of the most famous pop groups in England grew up in this area and were discovered when performing at the renowned 'Cavern'. The Beatles that were to have such an incredible effect on our youth culture and created a musical sound 'The Mersey Beat' that has become world famous.

The football teams – Liverpool and Everton are both Premiership teams.

When Daniel Defoe published his tour through the whole Island of Great Britain in the 1740's he wrote of Liverpool, which had begun as a row of fishermen's houses, was "very handsome, a London in miniature".

In 1800 the port of Liverpool which grew at the expense of Bristol had become the second largest city in the kingdom, priding itself not only on its elegant houses but also on its magnificent public buildings. In the 18th century Liverpool started to grow as the trade from the West Indies, Ireland and Europe flowed in and out of the port. The first wet dock in the world was built here in Liverpool in 1715. In 1846 The Albert Docks were opened by the man himself, Prince Albert and were known for many years as the modern wonder of the world. In 1880 Liverpool was granted city status and was hailed 'The Gateway to the Empire'. By the start of the 19th century forty per cent of the world's trade was passing through these docks. During this time not only did the docks grow in size and world status but many beautiful and majestic buildings were erected.

All this growth of the docks, erection of important buildings and its location near the sea has led Liverpool to be able to offer people anything they want. Whether you are looking for sand and sea, exciting shops, excellent cuisine, or just peace and quiet you will find what you are looking for when you visit Liverpool 'European

City Of Culture'.

Liverpool has grown in size and world status but this city also has a dark side. From its conception in 1107 to present day, it has witnessed much death and suffering from the times of Viking raiders, plague and Civil War when Prince Rupert laid siege to the town. In 1846 after the potato famine in Ireland, 300,000 Irish immigrants arrived. Disease was rife and led to 21,000 deaths in one year alone, one in fifteen of the population of the town died. This resulted in the appointment of the first Medical Officer Of Health in Great Britain.

During World War Two there were over eighty air-raids on Merseyside and in excess of two thousand five hundred people were killed. Perhaps all of this death and trauma has led to Liverpool becoming one of the most haunted cities in the country. During one of the air-raids on October 9th 1940 the famous Beatle John Lennon was born.

Merseyside is home to some of the most well known folk in the paranormal world - Derek Acorah the world's most famous medium, Tom Slemen ghost hunter and author, Steve Parsons and Ann Winsper of Parascience the best investigative paranormal group in England.

Derek Acorah.

Derek over the past ten years has achieved international success with his television and personal appearances across the United Kingdom, Europe, the Middle East and the U.S.A. He has conducted telephone consultations for people as far south as India, Australia, and New

Derek and Richard at Derby

Zealand. His early life was spent in Bootle, where he first discovered his psychic abilities and became interested in Spiritualism. It was during this time that he made contact with his spirit guide 'Sam', an Ethiopian from fifteen hundred years ago. He pursued a career as a footballer for many years, playing for Liverpool F.C. reserves, where he played alongside Emlyn Hughes and predicted the Liverpool captain would have a car crash—the day afterwards when Hughes had written off his car, Bill Shankly told Acorah to leave his psychic abilities at home and just play football. Derek has been involved with a number of television programmes and it was during the making of one of these that I came to meet and work with him. We had great fun travelling around this country and abroad and were very lucky to visit many wonderful historic and haunted places. Derek and I spent many long hours discussing why people haunt this world and do not move on. I learnt a great deal about the paranormal and ghosts and through our discussions we have forged a friendship not just between ourselves but between Ray his son-in law, Gwen his wife, and all our families.

Tom Slemen.

Tom Slemen is the leading authority on the ghosts of Merseyside, and is a well known personality in this part of the country. He is known best for his books on Haunted Liverpool of which there are at least fourteen in the series. His interest in ghosts started as a child when he lived on Melville Place, Liverpool. As a child he lived in a haunted house where his mother saw the ghost of a Victorian maid carrying a serving plate with the sound of children playing in the background. Having an inquisitive mind he tried to discover who this maid might be. During his research at the local library he discovered that their house stood on the site where an orphanage had once been. He then realised why a nearby street was called Orphan Street. As well as writing books he is a columnist for local newspapers and a radio broadcaster. After linking ghosts and history he became hooked on ghost hunting. I was lucky enough to make Tom's acquaintance when I visited Radio Merseyside to take part in one of his regular broadcasts. It was during this meeting that Tom told me about the haunting of Rodney Street .

So settle back, turn down those lights, and let me take you on a tour of haunted Merseyside.

PARA.SCIENCE

It was February 23rd, my birthday; I was conducting an investigation in Staffordshire. I walked into the building and was greeted by a new face who seemed to know me. He introduced himself as Steve Parsons from Para.Science. How's he got in here I thought? We soon got chatting about various aspects of the paranormal and much to my amazement every topic that I mentioned he also had a very sound knowledge. We talked about infrasound, the stone tape theory, the dead returning, EMF, the amazing amount of energy given off by the body and I then dropped one in that I thought would impress him; did you know that the brain continues to emit electro magnetic signals for 27 hours after death! "Yes I do" he said", but it's longer than that - it can be days after". "Oh" I said, "how do you know that"? "I used to be a nurse" he said. Then he dropped one on me, "did you know that the human body gives off about two kilo-watts of electricity every day", "wow" said I.

Even though he has seen a ghost just as I have, he is also a huge sceptic, as I am and believes as I do that at least eight out of ten ghosts can be explained.

After about half an hour of discussion I'm realising that he really knows what he's talking about. I'm also starting to think to myself, I reckon that I could work with this guy.

First off I needed to know more about Para. Science, who were they, what could they do and where did they come from? Guess what they are Merseyside's very own Paranormal Investigation Group.

Steve Parsons, founder of Para.Science

Para.Science was co - founded 12 years ago by Steve Parsons and Ann Winsper to examine paranormal activity using proper scientific methods of study; they now have members all over the UK drawn from all walks of life but especially from the medical profession.

The team can draw on over £86,000 worth of the very latest high-tech equipment to aid their investigations, (yes £86,000). They have the ability to observe and measure many of the environmental variables that are found and implicated in modern ghost hunting, ranging from temperature, humidity, electromagnetism, infrasound, ultrasound and even the earths own magnetic field.

All of this impressive equipment can only play a supporting role and can't replace the sound methodologies that Para.Science has developed over the years. All aspects of their cases are carefully researched and explored meticulously and they don't only look at the anomalies within the location but also carefully study the psychology involved.

Steve and Ann both have specialist areas of interest. Ann takes great care to record and document everything and anything that happens during an investigation and is a great believer in lots and lots of paperwork. Throughout the entire investigation the team have to fill in endless questionnaires and report sheets to help with the psychological data collection and so have to work very hard on every investigation they carry out. Steve is the groups 'gadget-o-holic' and is in his element when surrounded by all the 'gizmos' that they use. He has a strong interest in the measurement of the physical environment and physical phenomena and has developed several new methods for exploring haunted locations and trying to capture any unusual phenomena that may occur.

Ann is currently studying towards a degree in psychology, with a strong bias towards aspects involving parapsychology. Steve has recently commenced a PHD looking at temperature changes associated with paranormal reports.

To say that they were thorough would be the understatement of the year. While many paranormal groups do a ghost hunt in 24 hours Para.Science can take anything up to three years to complete an investigation.

Membership is by invitation only and I have recently been invited to join their ranks, I consider this a great privilege to be asked to become a member of what I believe to be one of the best paranormal investigation groups in the world.

1. THE GHOSTS OF PENNY LANE

Long before I came on the scene, number 44 Penny Lane had already been investigated by Tom Slemen and Derek Acorah who both witnessed a misty apparition which almost solidified into a contorted, distressed face. Derek stated that this was a manifestation of a man who committed suicide in the 1940's.

This lane was made famous when it was used as the title of the hit song Penny Lane written by Paul McCartney. The majority of my teenage years were spent working in the family record business and we sold more pop singles than anyone else in the Midlands. You can imagine the tremendous number of recordings we sold of the double-A- sided single of Penny Lane and Strawberry Fields Forever (written by John Lennon) in 1967. The fame of this pop group 'The Beatles' has resulted in Penny Lane becoming a place of pilgrimage for Beatle fans when visiting Liverpool. The street signs saying Penny Lane have become a memento for folk to take home with them and to combat their continual theft city officials have had to resort to painting the street names on the sides of buildings.

What better place to start my tour of Merseyside than Penny Lane that holds so many happy memories of my early working life. Little then did I know that my career change in latter years would bring me to this famous city but not in the search for music but in the search of ghosts!

The property reputed to be haunted is number 44 Penny Lane. The property in question, certainly since the 1930's has seen a lot of poltergeist activity emanating from it.

A family lived in the house next door to the haunted number 44. They moved in and within days they heard loud footsteps walking up and down the landing, and loud banging and clattering was heard by them during the day and night. The family became so fed up with the continual disturbances that they decided to go round and find out what was going on. They knocked on the door of the property several times, but no one ever answered. It went on day after day until they eventually called in the police. Mysteriously, the property was found to be empty, and the police said there were no squatters and there had definitely not been anyone living there for quite some time.

The family were so afraid by what the police said that they brought in a priest to exorcise the ghost, unfortunately it was to no avail and they moved out in desperation. Suddenly everything seemed to go quiet and the house remained empty until 1945. When another family moved into the property they had no sooner unpacked their bags when they heard creepy footsteps coming from the house next door but again on investigating nobody was there. They also made a hasty retreat from the building.

On completing research on the property it was discovered that the house had been bombed during the war. Are the footsteps and bangings made by some unfortunate tenant that met their untimely death when the house was blitzed?

The ghostly activity at number 44 now seems to have gone quiet but there have been reports of other ghostly activity in other buildings on Penny Lane. I visited a glass shop to see if I could get any more information on these hauntings and on talking to the proprietors they told me that unexplainable noises and poltergeist activity has taken place in their flat above the shop. They have heard the sound of breaking glass and furniture moves of its own accord. They also frequently sense the presence of a woman, who she is they do not know.

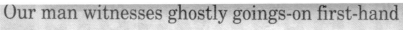

Our man witnesses ghostly goings-on first-hand

Showbiz pyschic unmasks poltergeist

I RARELY use psychics or mediums during my investigations into hauntings and paranormal phenomena, frankly, because I have never been impressed with people who profess to be in communication with the dead but can never produce a surname, just a "John" or a "Mary."

Many mediums I have encountered over the years have used little more than blatant hypnotic suggestion on gullible people genuinely seeking knowledge about loved ones who have passed "over to the other side".

'A misty form appeared in front of me'

However, last week I decided to give a psychic named Derek Acorah a try. He was literally a random choice, and when I asked if I could put him to the test by taking him to several well-researched haunted dwellings with a view to contacting a supernatural entity, Derek was very enthusiastic about the proposal.

I knew he was a busy man who is regularly consulted in Hollywood by showbiz celebrities such as Cher, Bette Midler, Demi Moore and a galaxy of other megastars.

I was therefore surprised to find Derek a typical down-to-earth Scouser who hadn't forgotten his tough Scotland Road upbringing.

The rendezvous was 44 Penny Lane, the abode of a particularly durable poltergeist — and also the premises of Property Line, a student accommodation agency.

I had made prior arrangements with manager Ronnie Kingsley to open the shop on Sunday, and as soon as Derek arrived on the premises he zeroed straight in on the small backroom of what had been an epicentre of terrifying poltergeist activity since 1930.

This room is now used as the shop staffroom.

INVESTIGATION ● Tom Slemen, right, meets pyschic Derek Acorah outside the 'haunted' shop in Penny Lane
Code JR2045

What followed next was both sensational and unexpected.

Derek gave me the name of a man who committed suicide at number 44 way back in the 1940s. The living descendants of the unfortunate man have asked me to refrain from giving his surname, so I have to comply with their wishes, but Derek not only revealed the man's name to me, he also told me the exact tragic circumstances of the man's suicide.

As Derek was standing in the room, a misty-looking form appeared in front of me and a witness, and almost solidified into what appeared to be a contorted, distressed face.

Derek calmly told me this was a manifestation

LOCAL MYSTERIES
with **TOM SLEMEN**

of the suicide which had taken the man's life, and the medium then claimed that his spirit guide "Sam" was present, overseeing things.

Seconds later, the eerie-looking face dissolved like a vapour, and Derek seemed very pale and drained.

When he had recovered back in the shop, he told me there were more earthbound entities present from different time periods.

He also warned me that the embittered suicide entity would become hostile because it had been disturbed and identified.

HARDWOOD WINDOWS. BUT THE ONE THING YOU ARE

2. BIDSTON ON THE WIRRAL

Bidston is a picturesque village situated on a hill sixty meters above sea-level and surrounded by one hundred acres of heath and woodland. Many historic buildings and mysterious rock carvings are to be found in this area, including a carving of a sun goddess. This carving is thought to have been fashioned out of rock by the Vikings around one thousand A.D. It was positioned to face the rising sun on mid-summers day the twenty first of June. At the time of the carving of this statue the sun was still thought to be all powerful and its life giving properties made it the supreme deity of these pagan people. Sun worshippers lit fires to increase the power of their prayers and these fires kindled on earth were also thought to increase the power of the sun which they worshipped. Even today many people cling to these superstitions which had their origins in the ore that every primitive farmer must have felt as the sun goddess made her miraculous daily march across the sky.

In 1771 a light house was built on Bidston Hill as it could be easily seen by ships to enable them to avoid the sandbanks in the channel. Wreckers from the Wallasey area would light beacons to confuse the captains causing their ships to founder. On stormy nights the locals watched eagerly for stricken vessels and ghoulishly swooped on wreckage and survivors who survival chances were considerably lessened by an ancient law --- it was illegal to claim salvage from a wrecked ship if any of the crew were still alive. This law virtually condemned these survivors to death. It is said that on a stormy night the cries of drowning sailors can sometimes be heard carried by the wind.

After the death of their parents in 1919 two sisters, Victoria and Margaret Webster, came to live in Bidston village after inheriting money and bought a terraced Victorian house. Victoria was twenty four years of age and her sister Margaret was nineteen. The two girls were very attractive and soon started to come to the attention of the young men living in Bidston. Victoria had a regular boyfriend called William and the pair often went out dancing leaving Margaret at home alone. One such night Margaret had retired to bed early when at about twelve o'clock she heard a noise downstairs. Thinking it was her sister and William returning home she called out to them and on receiving no reply she got up to see who was there. On reaching the stairs she saw a shadow pass across the bottom of the stairs. Margaret still thought that it was William playing one of his usual jokes to scare her. However, on still not getting any response to her calls she decided to go downstairs and have a look. On reaching the parlour she saw that the fire was still burning and realised she had forgotten to put the fireguard around it. On walking across the hall a figure wearing a Charles II type wig, a red velvet jacket and silver waistcoat passed in front of her. On looking closer Margaret saw his face which looked grotesque and turned to run away. The figure came in pursuit and eventually caught hold of her dragging her onto the floor tearing her nightdress whilst trying to kiss and fondle her. Margaret was able to reach out and grab the poker and started hitting the man repeatedly about the head. Eventually the man leapt up and ran off disappearing down into the cellar. Meanwhile Margaret's screams had come to the attention of the neighbours and also of Victoria and William who were returning home. They discovered Margaret covered in scratches, with blood on her face and clothing in disarray. She told her story but they did not believe her. They accused her of letting a local lad into the house. However, a few weeks later Victoria and William were returning from church when they saw the man that Margaret had described staring at them through the parlour window. They rushed into the house just in time to see the fellow concerned disappear down the cellar stairs. They followed him down into the cellar but no trace of him could be found. There was no other exit from the cellar. After this second sighting he was not seen again but the girls lived in fear of what might one day come out of the cellar. The door to the cellar from then on was always kept locked.

In the winter of 1922 pipes burst in the house and Margaret and Victoria had to call in the waterboard. In order to make the repairs the workmen had to dig under the cellar floor. It was during these excavations that an old coffin was uncovered. As a result the police were contacted and came to investigate. On opening the coffin it revealed a man wearing the identical clothing to the figure that Margaret had described as her attacker. In the bodies hand was found a book which closely resembled a bible but this book had an upside down pentagram on the front cover, the sign of a Satanist Unfortunately on contact with the air both book and clothing disintegrated.

Local historians thought that the body could be that of Richard Tilley who was a notorious Satanist, rapist and murderer who lived in the Wirral. He was reputedly tried and sentenced to death for murder but managed to escape from prison and disappear. It is believed that he may have come to live in the village of Bidston and inhabited the house of the Webster sisters where he died and was buried in the cellar.

Margaret and Victoria soon left the house and moved away to North Wales never to return to the village. What of Richard Tilley's mortal remains? He was refused a Christian burial and is buried somewhere near Bidston Hill in unconsecrated ground.

3. SPEKE HALL

Speke Hall which is situated on the North bank of the River Mersey, six miles from the centre of Liverpool and thought to be one of the most famous half-timbered houses in the country.

The building of this hall was started in 1490 but was not fully completed until the early sixteen hundreds. There had been a building on this site prior to this date. The origin of the word speke (spec) comes from the Old English word meaning brushwood.

The hall has changed very little in structure over the years with the exception of a few internal changes and some additions on the eastern side. In 1943 the hall was handed into the care of The National Trust.

Speke Hall was built and inhabited by the Norris family for

One of the best preserved timber framed houses in the country.

many generations. The Norris family were staunch Catholics and Royalists so this might account for there being a priest hole, secret passages and a built-in mirror in one of the bedrooms to allow the occupant to see the gates and warn any priests of danger. The North West of England was very pro Catholic and after Queen Elizabeth was excommunicated by the Pope it became high treason to be a Catholic priest. If found guilty you would be sentenced to death.

It was 1936 when the Beauclerk's family became the owners of Speke Hall, but because they mainly resided in their other properties down south the building soon became neglected and fell into a dilapidated state. The ghost stories seem to have originated around the time of the ownership of the Beauclerk's. Legend has it that Lord Sydney Beauclerk returned home one day with distressing news that the family had fallen into financial ruin. His wife was so traumatised by the news that she totally lost touch with reality, rushed to a window in the tapestry room through which she dropped her young child into the moat below. After committing this dreadful deed she killed herself in the great hall. Is the ghost seen walking through the walls of the hall Lady Beauclerk too frightened to move on fearing what might become of her in the next world. She had committed not only murder but also self murder in the eyes of the church and so was destined to burn in Hell for eternity.

After the Beauclerk's a local lad called Richard Watt bought the property. Adelaide Watt frequently saw a ghost disappearing through a wall in a bedroom. On further investigation in the area where the ghost disappeared through the wall a secret passage was discovered. Is it the ghost of Lady Beauclerk, or the ghost of a priest who frequently disappeared through the wall into a priest hole to avoid capture and certain death by hanging drawing and quartering. Perhaps we will never know. All we can be certain of is that Speke Hall is definitely haunted.

While I was completing my research for this book and D.V.D. I was talking to one of the renovation builders at the Bluecoat buildings in the centre of Liverpool. They did not have any ghost stories of Bluecoats but they told me of a university building, with a clock on it, near to the Catholic Cathedral, which was also undergoing renovation. One of the builders was in a room that had oak panelling on its walls that had been brought from Speke Hall. He was making a cup of tea when a lady in a long grey dress appeared in the room and he asked her if she would like to join him for a cup of tea. Her response was to vanish before his very eyes. Has the ghost of Speke Hall travelled with the oak panelling to this building in the centre of Liverpool?

4. BEBINGTON

Bebington Church

Bebington is a village steeped in history and a place where paranormal investigations are on going. Most of the ghostly phenomena always seem to focus around the village Church of St. Andrews. The present church originates from Norman times and was built of sandstone. Before this there was an earlier Saxon church built of wood . The church was at one time used for training novices of the priesthood. The young monks travelled between here and Chester in order to complete their training. There has been many reports of people seeing ghostly apparitions of monks walking from the church yard in the direction of Kirket Lane. There have been sightings of grey hooded monks sitting in the church pews exactly where the monks sat when they attended a church service. The

Headless monks, possibly vandalised by   Sunken road, Bebington Churchyard
Cromwell's troops

apparitions of the monks seen in the graveyard are often said to be headless or legless. On walking around the graveyard I came across a stone statue of four headless monks. Why they are headless nobody knows. Monks frequently seen wandering around this graveyard are reported to be legless. The reason for them appearing legless is that they are walking on the ancient track way that use to cut across the churchyard but was then eighteen inches lower than the ground level of today.

Up until its demolition in the 1930's Orchard Cottage stood adjacent to the church. The residents of this cottage often heard the sound of a galloping horse approaching their gates at great speed and stopping suddenly at the entrance to their drive. On investigating the residents never saw anything or found any tracks of a horse's hoofs on the ground. A bell ringer returning home one evening to Amesbury on his bicycle heard something galloping towards him. Nothing was visible although it was a clear moonlit night. Many folklore legends are based on the possibility that men and women often return in animal form, from that of the werewolf to the witches power to transform herself into a cat. Could this be an explanation for the sounds of the galloping horse, who knows?

5. POULTON ROAD, BEBINGTON

Poulton Road in Bebington is also reputed to be haunted by a religious ghost who is thought to be a young novice. In the 1970's a motorist saw a young girl dressed as a novice walking along the road. Being concerned for the young girl's safety he stopped and opened the passenger door to offer her a lift. The girl vanished before his eyes. A few weeks previous to this another motorist experienced the same apparition which also disappeared in front of him. There is a story of a young novice who had suffered a broken romance and as a result had decided to become a nun. She was walking along this road and disappeared, never to be found. Was she murdered? Or did she commit suicide? We will never know.

6. CLATTERBRIDGE HOSPITAL

Clatterbridge Hospital in Bebington started its life as a workhouse but today its original buildings have been demolished. Over the last fifteen years I have spoken to more nurses than any other members of the community who have provided me with so many ghost stories. Is this because they are dealing with life and death every day? Patients often tell of visits during the night from nursing staff who do not fit a description of any nurses working on the ward. Are these nurses so devoted to their place of work that they do not want to leave? Many hospital staff tell me that they often know when a patient is going to die because a loved one who has already passed on comes to collect

them. The dying person frequently smiles and seems to be acknowledging someone around their bed that only they can see. At Clatterbridge Hospital many staff have reported ghostly goings on. Sightings include those of medical staff and American soldiers --- this building was used as a U.S. hospital in World War Two. In recent years the activity has diminished as many of the Victorian buildings have been demolished.

7. LEASOWE CASTLE

Leasowe Castle

This castle was built in 1593 for the 5th Earl of Derby and was used as their summer home, however they did not upkeep the building and it fell into disrepair leading it to be known by the new name of 'Mockbeggars Hall', a name given to old, derelict and often haunted

The mirror in question.

manor houses and castles. Today it offers the chance for people to sleep in a haunted castle as it has been turned into a magnificent hotel. After filming at the hotel a film crew discovered distortion on a huge mirror which hung on the staircase. On returning to repeat filming of this footage they found hinges at the side of the mirror which supported a secret door. On opening this door they discovered a priest hole. The other ghostly apparitions are seen by people staying in room 22, The Earl of Derby suite. When this suite was being refurbished they were knocking down a wall in the bathroom when they discovered a secret room.

These ghostly sightings could be the wandering spirits of a father and son who were imprisoned at the castle as a result of a family feud. The father knew that they would be subjected to horrific torture at the hand of their captors and so to save his son from such a fate he smothered him with a pillow. After murdering his son he then committed suicide. When the castle became a hotel in the 19th century the room where the murder and suicide took place was converted into a bedroom. Many guests reported being woken in the early hours of the morning to see an apparition of a man and young boy standing by the window. Is this the father and son who met with such a sad demise years before?

Along the coastline from Leasowe Castle we find the origins of the legend of the Leasowe Mermaid. When seen she is sitting on boulders near the shore on evenings when there is usually a full moon. She is reported to be both beautiful and irresistible as one young man discovered to his cost. John Robinson was sailing his boat close to Leasowe shore when he was captivated by the mermaid sitting on the rocks. John had been warned by his mother of the tale surrounding this mermaid and that a sailor should never invite her on board. Disregarding his mothers warnings John was so captivated by her beauty and bewitching voice that he could not resist inviting her aboard his boat. The two talked for a long time and before returning to the sea the mermaid gave John a present of a ring. Five days later after this meeting John died of a broken heart. It is said that many other sailors have been swept away to their doom after encounters with this captivating mermaid. So if sailing around this coastline beware if you see a mermaid basking in the moonlight on the rocks, do not ask her aboard.

8. FORMBY

Formby today is a popular tourist attraction and owes its origins to the Vikings who came over in 960 A.D. from Ireland bringing with them myths and legends which came to be known today as Viking Sagas. One of these sagas or stories are about large black dogs.

The sand dunes around the coastline of Formby are reputedly haunted by a fearsome large black dog, called Trash. This dog is said to have red luminous eyes and anyone seeing this animal is said to die or lose a close member of their family. This particular harbinger of death gets its name Trash because of the sound it is said to make as it strides through the wet sand. In the 1950's a gentleman was taking a short cut across the dunes when he was confronted by a huge black dog. He lashed out with a wooden stick only to find that the

The sand dunes at Formby

stick went right through the beast. Shocked and shaken he turned on his heels and ran for home. On arrival at his destination he was devastated to discover that his father had died. This sighting and consequence only goes to add more credibility that these black dogs are harbingers of death and misfortune.

These black dogs are said to be about the size of a calf, with yellow or red piercing eyes. Different areas of the country have their own specific name for them. East Anglia have Black Shuck, Yorkshire have Padfoots and Barguests, Devon have Yeth Hounds and The Isle of Man have Moody Doo. Sightings of these harbingers of death are still being reported to this day by credible people --- are they really myths and legends --- try telling this to people who have lost loved ones after seeing one.

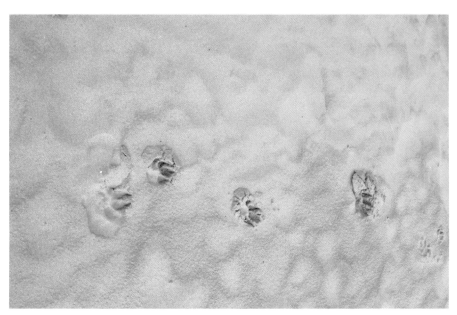

Formby sand dunes, could this be the footprints of Trash?

9. THURSASTON & THURSASTON HALL

In earlier times The Wirral Peninsula was a notorious haunt for smugglers and there are many tales of ghostly sightings and the sounds of tormented screams have been reported echoing from the gullies that join the high ground to the open sea. These sights and sounds are believed to be the tormented spirits of smugglers killed trying to avoid capture by customs men. Were these sightings true or false --- who knows. What better way to keep people away from areas where contraband is being delivered and hidden than to make up a ghost story of the surrounding area.

The area around Thursaston is marshland that is regularly filled by the River Dee. The name Thursaston is of Viking origin named

Thursaston village

after Thorsteinn a Viking farmer, and 'ton' being a farm or settlement. The other explanation for the origin of the name Thursaston is that it comes from Thorstone which is a large sandstone block linked to the Viking God Thor. It is quite a frequent occurrence for this stone to be struck by lightning during storms. The Viking settlers thought this to be the God Thor striking the stone in anger. During the Norman times the stone was also reputedly used as an alter where human sacrifices were made. In more recent times a witches coven were found to be using the stone for blasphemy and sacrilegious rights. However these practices were soon abruptly stopped by the police.

Thursaston Hall dates from 1070 A.D. and has been in the same family for over six hundred years. The hall is reputed to be the home of a number of ghostly apparitions of which the main one is of a white lady. She has been seen wandering around the bedrooms wringing her hands in despair and looking as though she is searching for something. This ghostly sighting has been linked to a previous owner of the hall who killed a young boy who was the rightful heir. The child was of a delicate nature and when his nurse returned from an outing to find him dead, suspicions about his death were not aroused. Years later when the lady was on her death bed she confessed to murdering the boy. The house was sold on her death and from then on people reported sightings of her ghost in the bedroom where the child was murdered. Due to these ghostly reports the bedroom was seldom used. However when an artist, Reginald Easton was attending a house party, he was given this room to sleep in because all the other rooms were occupied. His hostess was greatly concerned at allocating this room to Mr Easton but she made the excuse that the room was seldom used because of damp and draughts. However, Mr Easton replied he did not mind damp or draughts, but his host replied "that is not the problem with the room". Easton had also been commissioned to paint the portraits of his hosts daughters who were renowned for their beauty. Easton knew nothing of the murder or of the ghostly sightings when he retired to bed. In the early hours of the morning he was disturbed by an elderly lady standing at the foot of his bed. She looked very agitated and was ringing her hands in despair. He spoke to her where upon she abruptly vanished. The following day he relayed his sightings to his host who informed him of the murder of the young child. Undaunted by the truth Easton lay awake the next night waiting for the lady to pay him a return visit. She appeared again at the same time and continued to do so for the whole of his stay at the hall. When the lady appeared to Easton he grabbed his sketching pad and drew a sketch of the apparition. On completion of the sketch Easton showed the drawing to the family. They instantly recognised its similarities to a portrait of the supposed murderess but this painting did not hang in Thursaston Hall at this time. The painting was hanging in another property belonging to this family so Easton could not have cheated and copied a likeness from it. This painting was returned to Thursaston Hall and hung along side the sketch by Easton. This sketch is one of the very few drawings of a ghost and was featured in Lord Halifax's ghost book.

10. Croxteth Hall

Croxteth Hall

Croxteth Hall stands in five hundred acres of parkland and was the ancestral home of the Molyneux family, the Earl's of Sefton. They started to build the original house in 1575 and the family inhabited the hall until the death of the last Earl of Sefton in 1972 when the estate was granted to the City of Liverpool and turned into a park.

In 1702 4th Viscount Molyneux added the west wing which is by far the most impressive part of the house. In 1771 the 8th Viscount became 1st Earl of Sefton.

In the 19th century the family received vast amounts of money from their investments which enabled them to add some large extensions to the hall. The architect T.H. Wyatt was engaged for this purpose and he added a south and east wing to the building. In 1902-

1904 a huge north wing was designed by Jonn Macivar Anderson and so completed the fully equipped Edwardian mansion.

Croxteth Hall is reputed to be haunted. The kitchen has had many reported sightings of a cook who is thought to be going about her daily chores of cooking and cleaning. One day one of the staff was cleaning the window sill after the kitchens had been decorated. To do this she had to stand on a chair to reach to the back of the sink. While stood on the chair someone pushed her so hard on the shoulder that she fell forwards into the sink. Luckily she wasn't hurt but was very shaken particularly when she turned round to find no one there. She beat a hasty retreat to the 'mess room' for a cigarette to help her calm down. Is this the ghost of a previous cook at the hall that does not want to relinquish control of her beloved kitchen to someone else.

The haunted kitchen

The corridor that Richard made a rapid exit from.

During my search for ghosts I have fled many frightening situations but never as quickly as the exit I made from the kitchen area in this hall. I was in this building for about three whole minutes. I should have remained on a vigil for an hour, but on hearing the sound of foot-steps, and knowing full well that no other person was around. I made a rapid exit, never to return.

The Sefton's have reported seeing the ghosts of members of their family, for instance the 6th Countess of Sefton claimed she saw the ghost of her dead husband in their bedroom. Many other ghostly occurrences have been reported such as taps which have inexplicably turned themselves on, constant electrical faults for which no explanation can be found and items have disappeared or have fallen over and broken for no apparent reason. Cupboard and wardrobe doors have been reported to open mysteriously of their own accord. I have recently discovered that these doors, especially wardrobe doors are portals to another world allowing spirits to pass from one to the other. The attic rooms of this hall were once staff quarters and the sound of running footsteps and voices of maids are often heard. Shadows and figures are often seen in the principal corridor. The scent of strong tobacco is frequently smelt when no one has been smoking. Could all these ghostly apparitions, poltergeist activity and unexplained smells be the Sefton family who still inhabit the hall that they lovingly built and do not wish to leave.

When asked by people where is the most atmospheric and frightening building I have visited my reply is Croxtheth Hall. It is the attic area that I feel would be the most difficult place to stay on

One of the attic corridors.

my own. This is because the hall is a vast building made up of many long and meandering corridors and staircases that culminate in the attics. When up in the attics you seem to be isolated and alone with only your inner most fears and thoughts for company.

When I was on another of my visits to Croxteth Hall I met Raymond and Elda Lempereur. Raymond had lived and worked at the hall for many years serving as the personal chef to Lord Sefton with the help of Elda. One day Elda was walking along the Sefton corridor in search of Grace, the house-keeper when she heard what she believed was Grace talking to someone in one of the rooms. She called out "Grace is that you"? but got no reply. The voices continued but did not respond to Elda, she walked into the room expecting to see Grace. No one was there! Elda thought no more of this and she never did find Grace that day. A couple of weeks later

Elda was at one of Lord Setton's other properties called Abbeystead, talking to Grace about the previous time when she had been looking for her at Croxteth Hall and heard her talking but could not find her. Grace replied "I was out that day but I know who that would have been - it was the ghost. That is the room where maids would not work on their own, they always had to work in pairs because they frequently saw dark shadows and heard voices - when there was no one there".

Raymond and Elda Lempereur

A young boy dressed in Victorian clothes has been seen at the top of the stairs and Lord Sefton has been seen by work men in the building. Another sighting reported at the hall was seen by Arthur, the head gardener, who was returning to the hall one night when he

The area where Arthur saw his ghostly red coats.

saw an area of mist, although it was not a damp and misty evening. In the centre of the mist he saw a group of soldiers, all dressed in red with white cross belts. Arthur thought they were probably re-enactors – and he shouted to them "come on what are you still doing here at this time of night"? To which their response was to vanish. Arthur was very disturbed and frightened by his experience.

11. THE WIRRAL MUSEUM

Hamilton Square where The Wirral Museum is situated is one of the finest Georgian Squares in the country. The building is constructed from Scottish granite and local sandstone and was designed by local architect Charles Ellison in 1882. Its two hundred foot clock tower is

The Wirral Museum in Hamilton Square.

a well known landmark which is clearly visible from both banks of the River Mersey. The chimes of this clock have echoed around the town of Birkenhead since the clock was first set in motion by Elsie Laird, the young daughter of the Mayor of Birkenhead, shipbuilder William Laird in 1886. Around 1990 the building was chosen to be the home for a new museum. During the renovation stained glass was found hidden beneath plaster board. Victorian style wallpaper was pasted to the walls returning the building to its former glory.

Ghostly sightings have been reported by members of staff and the general public of which two are more often seen. These are the sighting of the figure of a man sitting on the bench close to the main entrance after the museum has been closed to the public for the day. The man sits quietly before disappearing before their very eyes. The other sighting that is often reported by security staff at night is that of a person seen walking along a locked off corridor on the CCTV. One evening this person was seen by two staff members viewing the camera screens before he disappeared out of the cameras field of vision. One of the staff remained to wait for the intruder to come into vision of the next security camera while the other security guard rushed to the floor to apprehend the intruder. The watching guard was unnerved when the man failed to come into sight. He radioed through to his colleague to warn him that the intruder may have slipped into a side room to avoid detection. On checking the corridor the doors were all found to be securely locked and he failed to find any trace of the man seen on camera. All attempts have failed to identify who the man could be and sadly the CCTV footage disappeared but not before several of the staff had seen and verified the sighting of the intruder recorded on film.

Other ghostly sounds that have been reported are the sounds of a party, glasses clinking and piano playing coming from the ballroom. Jim Wheelan, a member of staff, was closing up late one evening when he sensed a presence was with him in the ballroom. As he left he heard a sound like that of a woman's long dress swishing along the floor behind him. Needless to say Jim beat a hasty retreat. The Town Hall had been the centre of many celebrations and parties over the years. Could these sounds be ghostly echoes of happy events from the past.

A tragic tale connected with this building is that of a young girl called Nellie Clarke who had lost her father during the First World War. As a result Nellie went to the New Years party given by the Mayor for war orphans and their mothers at the Town Hall. To quote The Birkenhead News of January 14th 1925 *"Nellie appears to have thoroughly enjoyed herself. She laughed and gambolled with the other children as any normal healthy child might be expected to do and before leaving she received several toys including a doll to which she became very attached and christened Betty"*.

Nellie's mother commented at the party on Nellie's high spirits and how much she enjoyed herself. That night Nellie was murdered and on the following morning her body was found by a Mr Doran. Her face was frozen in terror and her body was huddled against a telegraph pole. Mr Doran felt her hand and it was ice cold. Nellie's mother had sent her daughter on an errand to the local shop . She

Originally Birkenhead Town Hall.

expected her back in a few minutes and when this did not happen she frantically went looking for her. During her search walking down Bedford Road, Nellie's mum thought she heard a voice call out "Mammy, Mammy". It was just like a wireless set when you take the head phones off and the sound gradually grows dimmer and dimmer. She could not account for this at all as her daughter was already dead. Nellie's ghost still haunts Birkenhead Town Hall where she spent the last few happy hours of her short life. To this day her killer has never been found.

12. BIRKENHEAD SHORE ROAD PUMPING STATION

Birkenhead Shore Road Pumping Station. (The Giant Grasshopper) This large building houses the pumps that evacuate the water from the Mersey rail tunnel that pass under the river. The upper part of the building today has been made into a museum while the lower part still houses pumps to remove unwanted water. A former railway worker met with a tragic death when he was killed after falling into the pumping pit. There have been many apparitions and disturbances reported which have been linked to this unfortunate workers death.

There are new theories being explored by Merseyside's very own Para.Science that water can hold a memory or a recording. Perhaps the water in the pumping station still holds a recording of the tragic death and certain people 'tuned in' to a particular frequency for some reason witness the event being replayed over and over again.

13. HOOTON PARK

The origins of the name Hooton originates from two Saxon words 'ho', meaning a point of land stretching into the sea - 'tun', a farm.

The giant Vauxhall car factory now stands on the site that use to be an aerodrome at Hooton Park. In Tudor times the Stanley family built a luxurious manor house on this site. This house remained in the ownership of the Stanley's and their relatives until the 19th century when it had to be sold to pay gambling debts. The hall was next sold to Richard Naylor who was a Liverpool banker and he added a huge clock tower nearly one hundred foot in height. Next to the hall was built a racecourse which was taken over by the armed forces during the First World War and used as an aerodrome.

To serve as an airfield accommodation was needed to house the numerous aircraft that were stationed there so four huge hangers were erected for this purpose. After the war it became Liverpool's first airport. However, the hall had been sadly neglected over the years and had fallen into such disrepair that it was past saving and had to be demolished. In 1957 due to defence cuts the aerodrome was closed for good. The site was bought by

Aircraft at Hooton Park

Vauxhall motors as the location for their car factory.

The reported ghostly sightings at Hooton Park seem to be linked to the time when the site was used as a military airfield. The most frequently reported figure is that of a man wearing a military great coat. This lonely figure is seen at night by security staff wandering along the airfields perimeter road that is still in existence today. He is oblivious to the living and when confronted by anyone he disappears before their eyes. The identity of this serviceman is still a mystery today even though reports have been put in Vauxhall's news letters and local newspapers to discover his identity --- but to no avail he still remains a 'John Doe'.

In the early 1980's two of the hangers were commandeered and made into a private military transport museum. From the first opening of this museum a figure dressed in flying kit was frequently seen wandering around the corridors of these hangers. Sometimes volunteers working at the museum would see this same figure entering one of the rooms but on following them to see if they need help no one is there.

In the 1940's a member of the ground crew suffered a fatality when he walked into a rotating propeller, but his ghost would not be dressed in flying kit therefore it is more likely that the ghost is one of the many air crew who were killed when their planes crashed during take off and landing during the two world wars. He is probably one of the many airfield ghosts who don't realise they are dead!

14. BIRKENHEAD PRIORY

Birkenhead Priory is the oldest building left standing today on Merseyside. The priory was founded in 1150 and was inhabited by Benedictine monks who cared for the welfare of travellers for over 400 years and were responsible for the first regulated 'Ferry Cross the Mersey'. It stands right next door to the Cammell Lairds Shipyard and is surrounded by heavy engineering and shipyards but still retains a small chapel and museum.

From the 10th-16th Century the Black Monks of St Benedict played an integral part in the aspect of English life --- religious, social and economic. Under King Henry VIII they nearly became extinct with the dissolution of the monasteries in the 1530's. Although the monks living in the priory were thought to be honest

Birkenhead Priory

Another view of Birkenhead Priory

and kind, this was not always the case. One of the priors had been a murderer and had undertaken a penitential pilgrimage to Rome before being professed as a monk at Birkenhead.

Ghost stories about monks and nuns abound in this country telling of them being bricked up while alive, beheaded, hanged and subjected to other traumatic deaths.

The ghostly sightings connected with this building is said to be that of a monk seen wandering around the premises by visitors and staff both day and night.

Close proximity of The Priory to Cammell Larirds Shipyard

15. CAMMELL LAIRDS SHIPYARD

This shipyard was the main employer for over 170 years in Birkenhead. Many famous ships were built and launched at this yard, including the Mauritania and the H.M.S. Thetis in which almost 100 lives were lost in very tragic circumstances in Liverpool Bay while she was undergoing sea trials. Over the years the shipyard was the workplace for nearly 500,000 men of which tragic accidents happened resulting in many fatalities happening in the building. It has also been the place of murders and suicides.

The ship-yard was built on land adjoining Birkenhead Priory which resulted in a large part of the monastery and town graveyard being excavated to make way for the huge dry dock. During these excavations many bones were disturbed and exposed.

Cammell Lairds Shipyard

Since 2004, the shipyard has been the location for a long term investigation by Para.Science. They were originally called in by staff members who reported many unusual and strange goings on especially in the area of the shipyard offices. Cold spots, the sound of footsteps, shadowy figures and apparitions were all reported. Most of theses sightings of figures are only seen fleetingly by people. However, the figure most often seen is that of a woman wearing green overalls.

One of the most active areas was a corridor near the board room where shadowy figures had been reported, people felt nauseas and frequently suffered with headaches. This was reported by staff at the shipyard and also by members of Para.Science. All of this supposed paranormal activity was eventually explained away, after months of investigation in the corridor it was found that very high emissions of E.M.F were being emitted from an electric switch board behind a wall near the kitchen.

Another area of supposed ghostly activity was the huge former draughtsmen's office where shadowy figures were reported and a sense of uneasiness was often reported. Again after months of meticulous investigation most of the paranormal activity could be explained away by infrasound emanating from the engines of ferries in the ship repair yard on the nearby River Mersey.

I have to tell you that they cannot explain away all the strange occurrences in this ship yard. The ongoing investigation at Cammell Lairds has revealed many hard to explain instances, such as the sounds of doors slamming, cold spots, the sound of footsteps walking

Haunted offices at Cammell Lairds

on the overhead gantries, and fluorescent lights coming on of their own accord in front of a B.B.C. film crew. It looks as if there are enough ghostly and paranormal reports to keep Para.Science employed for at least another two years at Cammell Lairds Shipyard.

16. WALLASEY CENTRAL LIBRARY

This building is associated with paranormal activity and reputed sightings of ghostly figures. Wallasey Central Library is visited by many people every day wishing to borrow books or just to have a quiet place to sit and read. One of the ghost stories connected with this building is one of a caretaker who looked after the building during the First World War. He was at work one day when he received the devastating news that his only son had been killed. So distressing was this that the man hanged himself in the main corridor. Since this suicide visitors and staff have frequently reported strange and unusual feelings when in this area of the building. The temperature drops dramatically even when the heating is on full and guide dogs become nervous and uneasy when they come through the entrance to this corridor. One such guide dog refused completely to enter the building no matter how much it was coaxed by its owner. A medium was called in some years ago to try and clear the library of the ghostly presence. He picked up on two spirits, one of which was the caretaker and another male spirit. The medium was able to assist the caretaker in moving on but the other male spirit refused his help and is said to still frequent the building. This male entity is fleetingly seen by people when they are browsing the book shelves. Perhaps he is someone who loved reading books and found the library a place of sanctuary.

17. RODNEY STREET

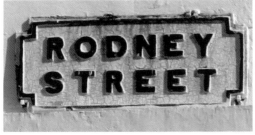

Rodney Street in Liverpool is said to be haunted by a fellow called James MacKenzie. He has been seen wandering this street at all times of the day and night by many folk one of these being a prostitute who reported him to the police. One evening she was approached by a well dressed gentleman wearing a top hat and cloak. Thinking him to be a potential client she acknowledged him and smiled. To her terror she realised that an approaching car headlights shone right through the gentlemans body. The man laughed at her terrified response and raised his hat and said "evening lassie". She took fright and ran screaming for her life in the opposite direction. Two men came to her aid believing her to have been attacked and escorted her to the nearest police station. When the woman was able to tell her story to the police they merely replied, "Oh you've just seen MacKenzie, love".

MacKenzie is said to have been a cruel, bad tempered fellow who gambled and lost his soul to the Devil. (To quote Tom Slemmon, Merseyside's own ghost hunter, author and broadcaster.)

The haunting of Rodney Street by this evil man originated in the autumn of 1871 when a respected doctor by the name of Dr Hartland was leaving his surgery on his way to visit a friend who lived on Blackburne Place. From the moment the doctor had turned

Rodney street

into Rodney Street he had felt very disturbed and a cold chill had run through his body although he was dressed in a heavy fur coat to keep out the evening chill. As the figure drew nearer he could see that he was wearing a top hat and a long flowing cloak. He was illuminated by the light from one of the street lamps. On seeing his face Dr Hartland became terrified when he realised that it was the face of a man he had known but had long been dead --- it was the evil Dr MacKenzie whom he had known twenty years before and who was said to be condemned to walk this earth without rest until Judgement Day. When this figure drew level with him it turned and said "Ha hospital Sunday". Dr Hartland knew that he was referring to a charity day that he held on Sundays to raise money for the needy people who could not afford medical treatment which they desperately needed. On looking into this evil face the Dr became even more terrified when he saw that its eyes were that of a dead person. Suddenly this figure turned and disappeared through the wall into the cemetery. After this experience Dr Hartland was feeling very shaken and unwell but managed to struggle to the house of his friend. On arrival at Blackburne Place he was taken in by his friend and given a brandy. After relaying his story, the doctor clutched his heart and fell back in the chair dead despite frenzied attempts by his friend to revive him. The last words spoken by the doctor was "tell Mr Brocklebank, he knows the story of MacKenzie".

This friend of Dr Hartland only knew of one man by this name, the millionaire ship builder Brocklebank. He wrote to this gentleman not expecting to get a reply. He was amazed when he was paid a *personal visit by this wealthy gentleman. Mr Brocklebank told the story of this man MacKenzie who made a fortune in railways and financed George Stephenson's Rocket. Although he was a respected member of the community he was known to be a compulsive gambler. The story tells of him having a sweetheart who died from a fever which resulted in him losing his faith and turning away from God who he blamed for her death. One evening MacKenzie became involved in a poker game with a gentleman by the name of Mr Madison. During this game MacKenzie gambled away all his money and possessions. Mr Madison said to MacKenzie if you do not believe in God then why not try and win back your fortune by betting with your last remaining possession --- 'your soul'. Sadly to say Mackenzie lost and was told by Mr Madison "Fear not, vain defeated one. I will not take your soul until you are laid to rest in your grave". When he turned to reply Mr Madison had disappeared.*

Before his death MacKenzie stated that he wished to be entombed in a pyramid above ground level and to be seated on a chair with a winning hand of poker. This was a desperate attempt to try and stop the Devil from claiming his soul by keeping his remains above ground.

I went in search of this haunted Rodney Street and the churchyard that contains MacKenzie's pyramid. On finding the location I discovered that the graveyard and church was boarded up. The only access was to climb over the wall but this was too high. I went in search of another entrance, when on turning the corner I met with a man selling hot dogs. At the side of his stall he had a plastic

Derek Acorah investigating the MacKenzie pyramid.

bread basket which I borrowed to aid me in my climbing of the wall. He said "if you do gain access to the graveyard and see a fellow in a top hat and cloak, remember me to him cos I've seen him loads of times". Once inside I found this incredible pyramid tomb containing the mortal remains of MacKenzie buried according to his wishes, sitting upright at a table with his winning hand of cards. Sightings of MacKenzie's ghost have been recorded by many different people --- from the milkman on his early morning rounds to the local 'bobbie on his beat'. Sadly to say, but with some relief I saw nothing of MacKenzie during my wanderings.

18. ARROWE PARK HOSPITAL

Arrowe Park Hospital.

"Is that your late wife, standing there

Beside your lonely bed.

Chiding you for mourning still,

When she has long been dead"

Sham Collins, 2000

Arrowe Park covers an area of approximately four hundred and twenty five acres. Around 1835 John Ralph Shaw built an Elizabethan style mansion called Arrowe Hall on this site. More recently a 910 bed hospital has been built on 15 acres of the land and today it provides a care centre for the physically and mentally handicapped. With the hospital being newly built and no other building on this area of the park before, and no reported battles and murders it appears that the ghostly stories must originate from the modern hospital.

There are regular reports of paranormal activity and ghostly apparitions being seen and heard in this hospital. The electronic nurse call system is frequently used when the rooms are not being used by patients. This building is centrally heated and climate controlled but all too often staff and patients report of sudden icy chills and drops in temperature with no explanation other than paranormal. However, the area that is reported to be the most haunted is the main operating theatre. Hardly a month goes by without one of the operating staff reporting some form of ghostly activity. Heavy fire doors that cannot move on their own frequently swing open and footsteps are heard on the corridor but no one is there. The most disturbing story is that reported by staff seeing a young girl calling for her "mummy" but when they go to her aid she disappears!

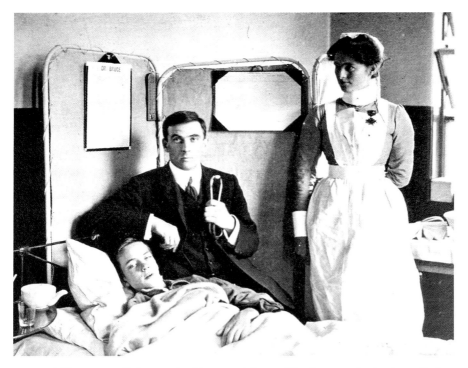

Whenever I have dealings with staff who work in hospitals, whether they be surgeons, nurses, cleaners, porters or para-medics, they frequently tell me of some paranormal or ghostly experience they have encountered while going about their everyday job. Is it no wonder that hospitals are haunted because of the number of deaths and trauma that they see every day. Theses reports and sightings are from credible people who have nothing to gain from making up ghost stories.

One incredible story that I was told was by a twenty two year old lady whose mum died when she was only eleven years of age. Her father had been diagnosed with terminal cancer and had been moved into a side ward for his last few days. A workmate of her father came one evening to say his goodbyes and as he approached the curtain around the bed he heard a familiar voice, one he had not heard for eleven years. He recognised this voice as the voice belonging to the dying mans dead wife. She was telling him "not to go as his children still needed him" and guess what against all odds he survived and is still alive today in remission --- explain that if you can!

Hospitals cannot be investigated for their paranormal activities due to the nature of their role in society and the sensitive part they play in our lives - perhaps sometimes things are best left alone.

19. LIVERPOOL CATHEDRAL

Liverpool is unique in having not one but two cathedrals both being constructed quite recently. The Roman Catholic Cathedral of Christ the King consecrated in 1967 and Giles Gilbert Scott's Anglican Cathedral which was started in 1904 and completed in 1978. It is the largest Anglican Cathedral in the world. It has the highest gothic arches, the largest organ, the heaviest ring of bells and its stained glass windows are the biggest in England.

It also has one of the scariest graveyards that I have ever been in now called St James's Gardens. This area of ground was once an important quarry from which the stone for many of Liverpool's public buildings was quarried. It became the main cemetery for Liverpool from 1825 to 1936. It was designed by John Foster Jnr the Liverpool architect responsible for many of the well known landmarks in the city. This cathedral is also unusual as it has a spring in its grounds. This spring was discovered in 1773 and its waters are considered to have medical properties for helping such ailments as stomach problems, nervous disorders, rickets and weak eyes. Today water is thought not only to have healing properties but it is also thought to have recording properties. This is where incidents often traumatic might be absorbed by the water in the same way that photographic paper, silicone in recording tapes can retain images. Is this why so many hauntings are associated with wells, streams, marshland, bathrooms, and springs?

The grave yard of this Anglican Cathedral is also well known

Liverpool Cathedral

The graveyard at Liverpool Cathedral.

because it contains the remains of William Huskisson. He has the distinction of being the first person in the world to be killed by a train. Huskisson was attending the opening of the Liverpool and Manchester Railway when he stepped off the train to greet The Duke of Wellington at the same time as Stevenson's Rocket approached on the parallel track. There was insufficient room for Huskisson to get out of the way of the train and it resulted in his leg being crushed. He was taken by the very train that had injured him (The Rocket) to Eccles, which was driven by the designer himself - George Stephenson. However, the trauma of the accident and the resulting injury proved to be too much and Huskisson died a few hours later. The successful career of Huskisson was brought to a traumatic end. He had held the post of Under Secretary at War, he had represented Morpeth as their member of parliament, and was appointed president of the board of trade and treasurer of the navy in 1823. Huskisson was laid to rest in the graveyard of this cathedral but doesn't seem to be at rest as there have been many reports of a ghost seen around his monument. In 1836 'The Huskisson Mount' was designed by John Foster Jnr, to house a statue of this great man. When I visited the grave yard, I hasten to add that this was in the day-time, as you certainly would never get me there at night. I noticed that there was no statue inside the monument. Is the ghost that of William Huskisson still lingering waiting for his promised statue?

The Huskisson Mount with no statue inside

20. THE MERSEY TUNNEL

The Mersey Tunnel has been excavated out of sandstone and clay and in many parts are actually below the water table which can create problems with drainage.

The haunted story relating to the Mersey tunnel is one of a young female hitch-hiker. One morning when driving to work a young man noticed a young girl standing in the tunnel looking lost. On his return journey he was very perplexed to see this young lady in the same area of the tunnel. He stopped his car and opened his passenger door to see if he could be of any help. Much to his amazement on opening the car door the girl vanished in front of him.

On relating his story to other folk he discovered that the B.B.C. Radio Merseyside between November 2000 and January 2001 had

The Mersey tunnel

Inside the haunted tunnel

been inundated with reports of a phantom hitch-hiker in the tunnel. One such report was of another young man travelling through the tunnel on his scooter. On coming upon the female hitch hiker he stopped and offered her a lift. She climbed onto his scooter taking up his offer of putting on his spare crash helmet. He felt the girl on the back of his scooter holding tightly around his waist. However, on reaching the end of the tunnel he stopped to let the girl get off and when he turned around no one was there. So when travelling through the tunnel keep your eyes open for this lost traveller and the choice is yours if you want to stop and give her a lift. Our taking photographs of the tunnel was very difficult and dangerous but a very kind Liverpool city policeman stopped to help. He allowed us to park by the tunnel and kept a watch on our vehicle while we completed our filming and pictures.

21. THE ADELPHI HOTEL

Staff at this hotel have had some unusual experiences. One such member of staff was awoken about five o'clock in the morning . The lady in question had only just taken up a position at the hotel and was actually staying for her first night. On opening her eyes she saw the figure of a man standing at the foot of her bed. After a fitful nights sleep she reported her experience to other staff in the morning only to be told "don't worry it is only George".

It is very common for ghosts to be given a nick - name as it gives them the status of a member of the family and it takes the fear out of the situation. This is always the best thing to do when a person is seriously upset by their first encounter with the paranormal. It may not be scientifically accurate but it is good psychotherapy.

The Adelphi Hotel

22. THE BLUE COAT SCHOOL

The Blue Coat School

The Blue Coat School was originally founded by a Reverend Robert Styth and financed by a man called Bryan Blundell in 1708. Blue Coat schools were set up around the country at this time as there was an urgent need for children to be cared for and to be given the chance to learn to read and write. They were given the name of 'Blue Coat' because it is the colour of alms charities. Blue was also the most used colour for clothes in Tudor times and so the school uniform consisted of blue frock coats and yellow stockings. This was the colour of the school uniform until 1948.

The Blue Coat building is one of Liverpool's most distinctive buildings situated in the heart of the city. It is an elegant Queen Anne grade one listed building with a cobbled courtyard and secret garden which makes it a must for any tourist visiting Liverpool.

When this first became a school it was able to accommodate fifty boys and by the early 1800's it was home for over three hundred. Sadly in 1941 the building was badly damaged in the Merseyside blitz. In 1949 the Bluecoat Society for the Arts began to restore the building and was completed in 1951. Whether it is the structural change of a building that disturbs spirits or whether old school boys long since dead do not want to see their school building changed we start to hear of paranormal activity.

At the top of the building there are reports of visitors hearing the cries of children who sound distressed. This room was thought to have been used as the punishment room for the children. Throughout the school there have been sightings of children and poltergeist activity has been seen in the format of doors opening and closing on their own. The stock cupboard door is found open when it has been firmly secured --- is a hungry child in search of food?

In 1899 it was realised that the building was no longer adequate and could not provide all the needs of the school and so the trustees took a major decision - this was to move the school away from the overcrowding of the busy city centre to the countryside of Wavertree. The building of the new school started in 1903 and was completed in 1906. However, there are still reports of poltergeist activity and sightings of children in the old school building --- are these the spirits of children who were glad of the chance of regular meals and an education and do not wish to leave their beloved school?

LIVERPOOL'S HAUNTED THEATRES

Theatres, cinemas and places of entertainment seem to attract more than their fair share of ghosts. At the end of every night when the applause has died down, the final curtain is closed, the lights are switched off and the audience go home the theatres become quiet and dark. However, this is not for long as this is the time when many of the famous entertainers return from the shadows to perform their favourite part over and over again. Is it the energy of the audience and the players that awaken these ghosts drawing them back to the atmosphere that they once loved?

23. ROYAL COURT THEATRE

The origins of this theatre go way back to the 12th century when folk used to congregate at this site as they drew their water from the well situated here. This site has been the home of many different forms of entertainment. In 1826 it was the home of the Cookes New Circus and in 1830 it housed Cooks Royal Amphitheatre of the Arts. In 1881 it adopted the name that it still has today and that is The Royal Court Theatre. Disaster struck the building in the form of a fire in 1933 which totally destroyed the building but there were no recorded deaths.

In 1938 the theatre was rebuilt in a totally new Art Deco style. The interior was given a nautical theme reflecting the sea faring origins of Liverpool. The basement lounge was given the same layout as the one on the famous Queen Mary. This brought back uneasy memories of my experiences in cabin 340 when I had been part of paranormal investigations on the Queen Mary in Long Beach.

The theatre has a more ominous side and has been the subject of folk experiencing paranormal and ghostly experiences when in the building. Staff report of hearing unusual noises coming from many of the rooms. This is only 'the tip of the iceberg' with poltergeist activity moving objects on frequent occasions. A figure has been seen in the main seating area when the building is not open to the public. On another occasion a maintenance man was sorting out some scenery screens on the main stage when his attention was drawn to a lone figure sat up in the stalls. Much to his dismay she

Royal Court Theatre

vanished before his eyes.

On one of my previous visits to this theatre I was involved in a table tilting session which took place on the stage. We had placed a bowl of water on the table when suddenly the table started to move violently spilling the water everywhere until the table managed to unseat me from my chair. I fell backwards and was very disturbed by what appeared to be a very strong spirit that seems to not want to leave the building. Who could this spirit be? A caretaker named Les is thought to be this resident spirit and frequently gets the blame for paint pots being upturned. During a winters day Les had gone up onto the roof to clear out some blocked grids when he lost his footing and slipped resulting in him breaking a leg. Despite crying out for help no one heard him and he died from shock and exposure.

On the site of an ancient well.

24. THE EVERYMAN THEATRE

The building that is home to this theatre was once a chapel of which some of the original features can still be seen. The ghost that frequents this place is most unwelcome but not for the unpleasant frights that it gives visitors and staff. It is the unpleasant aroma that it leaves behind. The smell is that of urine and no matter how much effected areas of the building are fumigated the stench cannot be removed. Staff often see dark shadows in the men's toilets when they are locking up, but there is no one their only this aroma for all to smell. Hand driers switch themselves on and off and lights frequently flash although all the power supply to them have been turned off.

25. THE LIVERPOOL PLAYHOUSE

Liverpool Playhouse

In 1999 the theatre was refurbished and work men were often disturbed when going about their daily jobs. One of the electricians was working on the buildings wiring when he reported several creepy experiences such as taps turning themselves on, heavy doors slamming too on their own. Whilst working in the basement he felt a 'presence' of someone watching him. The main ghost reported to haunt this theatre is one of a lady called Elizabeth who was a cleaner in the building in 1897. At this time the venue had not been granted a licence and was a music hall and variety theatre. Elizabeth was cleaning up on stage when the fire iron came loose and struck her. The blow knocked her off balance causing her to fall into the orchestra pit, breaking her neck in the process. Her death was recorded as accidental but the disturbing fact was that the fire iron was water powered and had to be operated by someone. Elizabeth's ghost haunts the building. Is she looking for the person who caused her untimely death or is she going about her daily work not realising she is dead?

Another ghost thought to inhabit the theatre is that of a man wearing a frock coat and top hat. The story goes that his daughter ran away to join a repertory theatre in the early 1900's and he is searching for her in the vain hope that he can take her home.

26. THE LIVERPOOL EMPIRE

The staff working at this theatre often report seeing the ghost of a young Victorian girl thought to be about ten years of age. The sightings of this young girl are spread over many years and she is most often seen late at night when the building is being closed. People are not certain of whom she is but there is a rumour that a young girl fell to her death from the circle into the stalls below.

So when next visiting a theatre keep alert you might see a handyman but is he real? If you smell the stench of urine don't take too long in the toilets --- hurry back to your seat because you never know who might be watching.

The Liverpool Empire.

27. ST GEORGE'S HALL

This hall is frequently called the jewel in Liverpool's crown because of its magnificent architecture. It has been described as the finest Greco-Roman Building in Europe. It is situated in Lime Street, Liverpool and is used today for many private and public functions. During its history St George's Hall has been visited by many famous dignitaries and royalty. Queen Victoria on such a visit said *"It is worthy of ancient Athens, the architecture is so simple and magnificent. It is well raised and approached by a splendid flight of steps --- the interior is quite unfinished, but will be very fine, the taste so good and pure"*.

The hall opened its doors to the public in 1854, ten years after it had first been commissioned and designed by the architect Harvey Londsdale Elmes. The cost of erecting this building was £300,000 and its organ, a Henry Willis, is regarded as being one of the finest in the country with a total of seven thousand, seven hundred and thirty seven pipes. Up until the building of the Albert Hall it was considered to be the largest pipe organ in the world. Incorporated in the structure of the building was an air conditioning system considered to be the world's first. A female building supervisor was on the stairs in the vicinity of the organ when she was pushed firmly in her back nearly sending her falling down the stairs. Feeling angry and disturbed she swung round to confront the person responsible for this dangerous prank, only to find no one there! Other reports have been made by people in this area who have felt uneasy and seen what they believe to be dark shadows out of the corner of their eyes. Are these ghostly feelings and uneasiness explained by the huge air vents within the building causing infra sound which have been proven by paranormal investigators to cause unease, a sense of fear and dark shadows. Who knows?

This building over the years has been a place for many rallies and gatherings. The deaths of Beatles John Lennon and George Harrison were commemorated here and the homecomings of Liverpool and Everton football teams after football victories have returned here.

However, this magnificent building has had a sad part to its history as it has been the home of the assize courts which are still preserved today along with their prison cells. Many famous murder trials were held in these courts and from here folk were sentenced to

St George's Hall

death or life imprisonment. One such lady was Florence Maybrick, a young American woman who was convicted of poisoning her English husband James with arsenic. However, during her trial she was condemned as much for her adultery as she was for murder by the judge . This judge who passed the death sentence on Florence died himself not long afterwards in a lunatic asylum. The public executioner at this time was a man called James Berry and he confidently awaited the commission to execute her and pasted reports of the case into his voluminous cuttings book. Awaiting her execution Florence Maybrick was placed in Liverpool's Walton Gaol from where she could hear the erection of her own gallows.

When the American Civil war broke out in 1861 Liverpool had pro Confederate sympathies and Birkenhead's ship yard was building ships for the southern states, one of which was the CSS Alabama.

Florence was a great niece of Jefferson Davis, the Civil War leader of the Confederates, which no doubt played a large part in the American President Benjamin Harrison asking for clemency on her behalf. A reprieve was granted due to the American pressure and public opinion here in England and the executioner Berry had to cross her out of his appointment book! As a result of this reprieve a popular street ballard was composed and published.

"But Mrs Maybrick will not have to climb the golden stairs;
The Jury found her guilty so she nearly said her prayers;
She's at another kind of mashing and at it she must stop,
Old Berry is took down a peg with his long drop".

Another of the infamous murder trials that took place in St.

George's Hall is that of Charles Connolly, 26 and George Kelly, 27. They were accused of the brutal murder of the manager of The Cameo Cinema and his deputy who were both shot at point blank range when counting the takings for the day. The pair stood trial on the 12th of January 1950 before the judge Roland Oliver. The prosecution alleged that George Kelly was the gun man and that Charles Connolly had acted as look-out. However, after one of the longest murder trials in British history the jury failed to reach a verdict and a retrial was ordered. Kelly was found guilty and later executed at Walton Gaol by Albert Pierrepoint. Connolly was imprisoned until 1957 and died in 1997. Shortly before his death he took part in a B.B.C. radio interview, which he reaffirmed both his and Kelly's innocence. Their case was taken before the Court of Criminal Appeal in February 2001 and in June 2003 Kelly's and Connolly's conviction were thought to be unsafe and squashed. As a result Kelly's relatives had his remains removed from their prison grave and given a dignified funeral in Liverpool's Metropolitan Cathedral. Perhaps he can rest in peace now justice has prevailed. The most haunted part of this building is thought to be the stair case leading from the 'dock' down to the cells. Perhaps this haunting will slowly wain as Kelly finally got justice and closure in the end.

Ira and William Davenport were two American 'cabinet' mediums who in the 1860's astounded audiences on both sides of the Atlantic by apparently materializing 'spirit hands' that untied difficult knots and played musical instruments. In the advertising literature for the performance of the Davenport brothers they boasted 'musical instruments are made to play in the most extraordinary manner, and in the most profound and mysterious way'. Human hands and arms become visible, and many other interesting experiments are presented, originating only with the Davenport Brothers in the year 1855 and never produced with success by imitators. Sceptics are specially invited to be present and occupy front seats. Many spiritualists believed they were helped by ghosts and although professional magicians were able to prove that everything they did was just a conjuring trick they still managed to remain popular. However, one day whilst performing at St George's Hall they were exposed by a Birkenhead docker. This gentleman had tied the brothers up by using a 'Tom Fool' knot and placed them inside their cupboard from which the brothers were unable to release themselves and so no spiritual musical performance was given. This

Ira and William Davenport with their alleged spirit hands.

resulted in a very disillusioned audience and the brothers were 'hounded' out of the city of Liverpool.

In the bowels of this building are the prison cells with a cottage style of rooms that was once the home of the prison warder and his family. This area is reputed to be haunted. Visitors and staff have reported hearing the sounds of children emanating from this part of the building. St George's Hall has not been altered over passing years and is still easily recognizable to visitors today.

On April 23rd 2007 (appropriately St George's Day) the hall was reopened by Prince Charles after a twenty three million pound restoration during this year of Liverpool's eight hundredth birthday celebration.

28. THE FISHERMENS REST.
THE OLD PALACE HOTEL

The Old Palace Hotel, Southsea, was built in 1866 and contained some seventy five bedrooms and magnificent reception rooms. However, when the erection of the building was completed to the architects dismay they discovered that the hotel had been built facing the wrong way. Instead of facing out to sea it faced inland. This discovery was too much for the architect, William Magnall, that he reputedly committed suicide by jumping off the roof of the hotel.

The Palace Hotel built to grand designs in 1866

The lifts in the hotel were often reported to be heard moving up and down of their own accord when the building was being demolished even though there was no longer an electricity supply to the building.

It took me a considerable time to find the site where the hotel had stood and I was about to give up my search when I discovered a road called Palace Road. Before coming to find this hotel the only ghostly story I knew of was the one of the hotel lifts working on their own. I came to the site of a pub, The Fishermens Rest and my attention was drawn to a plaque on one of the walls which said:

"On such a night in the distant past
the surf raised high on the beach
the mexico bargue on a bank was fast
no port that night would she reach
three lifeboats to her aid were sent
by fishermen manned with good intent
one boat returned a crew to save
the others were drowned in a terrible gale.

Some of the Lifeboat crew.

This place they brought them here to rest no man can do more than

to give of his best

a nation mourned and mourning new pride

the pride of a nation in vain not died".

The Fishermens Rest is all that remains today of The Old Palace Hotel. This building was once the coach house and stables of the Victorian hotel. On the 9th of December 1886 there was a terrible tragedy at sea when a ship called 'The Mexico' floundered and crew from three different life boats were sent to her aid. This was the

The Mexico Barque

greatest lifeboat disaster in history. One of the lifeboats called 'The Eliza Fernley' of Southport lost 14 of their 16 man crew. 'The Laura Janet' of St Annes tragically lost all 13 of her crew. The bodies, twenty seven in all were all brought to the hotel and the area that is now the pub served as the mortuary. Most of the lifeboat men were fishermen by trade. Many of the crew who lost their lives were married with children. On entering the pub I met the manager who told me that the pub is named after these dead sailors that were brought here, hence it is called The Fishermens Rest. The manager told me he has heard stories from previous landlords of noises coming from the cellars when no one is in them. He had also heard that when the hotel was being demolished the lifts continued to go up and down without an electricity supply and continued to do this even when pounded by the workmens lump hammers. The lifts eventually collapsed and crashed down into the area of the building which is now the pub cellar. With such a tragic history no wonder this place is said to be haunted.

After completing our research on The Old Palace Hotel, we came across new evidence and research which had been completed by a group called M.A.R.A (Merseyside Anomalies Research Association.) They discovered that the architect thought to have committed suicide actually died of consumption on 29th May 1868 which is 2 years after the completion of the hotel. This proves that he did not jump off the roof of the hotel M.A.R.A also believe that the hotel was not built the wrong way round but was built facing inland to protect the reception area of the hotel from the coastal elements.

The extensive research of M.A.R.A. also revealed that Florence Maybrick and her husband James stayed at the Palace Hotel weeks before she poisoned him and a witness that was at the hotel at the time stated at the trial in St George's Hall that Mrs Maybrick was heard to say that she hated her husband.

During the Second World War the hotel was taken over by The American Red Cross as a rehabilitation centre for the U.S. Air Force.

In 1961 the body of a little girl was discovered in a bedroom directly opposite the lift shaft of the hotel. The number of the room was 13. After this tragic discovery the bedroom was sealed off and never used again. In 1963 a chamber maid reported seeing a little girl in one of the bedrooms and although asked who she was, she never spoke. The chamber maid was told that the room in question was

Coach house of The Palace Hotel, now the Fishermens Rest.

not occupied and there were no children in the hotel at the time.

In 1967 Boris Karloff made his last film called 'The Sorcerer', and 'The Haunted House Of Horror' was also filmed at this hotel just before it closed down in 1967.

In its hay day the Old Palace Hotel boasted hot and cold water in all bedrooms with state - of - the - art bathrooms. However, little remains of this once grand hotel that had on its guest list such famous people as Clarke Gable and Frank Sinatra.

29. LIVERPOOL'S HAUNTED PRISONS

Walton Prison was located just down the road from Kirkdale Prison and although they both had their own execution sheds they actually shared the same gallows that were transported from one to the other when required.

An execution shed.

Walton Prison was built between 1850 and 1854 which at this time made it one of the most modern prisons in the country. When Kirkdale was closing down in 1890 they marched the prisoners from their cells along North Dingle Lane and into their new home in Walton Prison and to our knowledge without loss of prisoners. Both of these prisons are reputed to be haunted. Kirkdale by the ghost of Catherine Flanagan who was hanged along side her sister for poisoning her brother-in-law Thomas Higgins with strychnine and three other victims. Why only Catherine's ghost is said to haunt and not her sister no one knows, but her ghostly shade has been seen by inmates and prison officers alike. The sisters were executed by Bartholomew Binns who was renowned for not being very good at his job. In March 1884 Binns was criticised for an inefficient execution at Walton Gaol, when the victims heart continued to beat for a quarter of an hour after the drop. The governor of the gaol in his opinion said "Binns had no idea how to do his work properly. He put the rope around the culprits neck and hanged them, but it was by accident whether the hanging was successful or not". Clearly this man would not do and another was appointed in his place. Could this be the reason Catherine Flanagan haunts this gaol --- did she suffer more than necessary at the hands of this bungling executioner?

James Berry was the hangsman who followed in the footsteps of Binns and one of his first victims at Walton Prison was a ironically a lady by the name of Mrs Berry, but she was not related to him, but was known to him. Berry had once danced with her at a police ball. Mrs Berry was now to die at his hands for poisoning her young daughter for the ten pounds insurance money. Whilst checking for signs of death in the execution pit Berry cut two locks of the woman's 'beautiful chestnut tresses' to keep as a souvenir. He had a macabre collection of relics from his victims which he kept as gruesome reminders of his work in his own home. One day Berry

A typical execution shed.

became disturbed by these relics particularly after the locks of Mrs Berry's hair joined his black museum. Berry felt sure that her ghost had travelled with them.

"I used to keep these relics, but they made me uneasy after a time, and one day I decided to sell them, though I had many of them from the day I started the business of public hangman. And believe me or not, it was a different house, was ours, when they were gone. I found I could sleep. There was no more weary tossing about in bed at night, and the uncanny feeling I used to have when I entered the room in

127

which they were kept disappeared. It was strange, but it may be that some of the evil influence of my victims clung to these relics".

The ghost at Walton Gaol is believed to be that of William Kennedy who was reputed to have murdered a policeman by shooting him in both eyes causing instantaneous death. However, my research has drawn a 'blank' with finding any person by the name of William Kennedy being executed in Liverpool during the twentieth century. One of the cells is haunted by someone or something. A dark shadow loiters at the bottom of the prison bed. This causes so much distress to the prisoner staying in the cell that they demand to be moved even if their only option is to be placed in solitary confinement.

Berry was a confident and skilful hangsman making very few mistakes until one day the interference by the Kirkdale's prison surgeon Dr Barr who disputed the length of the drop. When hanging a man by the name of John Conway, Berry calculated it to be four and a half feet, while Dr Barr insisted that it should be six foot and nine inches. A heated argument started in front of the terrified victim which led to them agreeing to reduce the drop by nine inches, Berry replied "all right I will do as you like but if it pulls his head off, I'll never hang another"!

John Conway stood shaking and shouted "hold on, hold on, I want to say something".

Berry replied "you can't say anything now it is too late".

The Catholic priest took Berry's arm, and the hangsman said in a temper, "G'et out o't way and mind your own business". The white

James Berry who executed many Merseyside people.

cap was lifted from Conway's face and he made a statement thanking the prison officials and forgiving his prosecutors. Berry re-arranged the cap, adjusted the noose and pulled the lever. The spectators immediately heard a loud squelch instead of the usual thud in the pit below. Berry shouted "Take 'em out, take 'em out" and rushed out of the room himself. It was Dr Barr who saw that Conway's head was hanging from the body by little more than a string of tissue, and that the pit was splashed with blood.

Berry hanged one or two men in the months following this disastrous event without any further mishap. However, it resulted in the following letter to the Home Secretary.

Dear Sir,

I herewith tender my resignation as executioner of Great Britain. My reason is on account of Dr Barr interfering with my responsible duty at Kirkdale Gaol, Liverpool, on the last execution there. I shall therefore withdraw my name now as being executioner to England. Trusting this will be accepted by you on behalf of the Sheriffs' of England, I remain, dear sir

Your obedient servant,

James Berry,

Late executioner of England.

On Thursday 13th August 1964 Peter Anthony Allen stood on the trap door of the gallows of Liverpool's Walton Gaol --- at exactly the same time – 8.00 a.m. in Manchester his accomplice in murder,

Gwynne Owen Evans stood likewise on a trap door --- both going down in history as the last two men to be hanged in the United Kingdom.

NO WONDER LIVERPOOL'S GAOLS ARE SO HAUNTED!

FURTHER RESEARCH

After reading this book you may wish to settle back in your arm chair, turn down the lights and follow in the footsteps of Richard as he completes his Haunted Tour of Britain on DVD.

Ghosts of The Isle of Man DVD

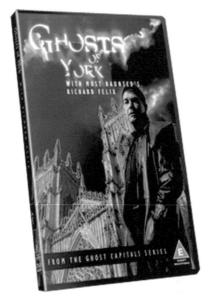

Ghosts of York DVD

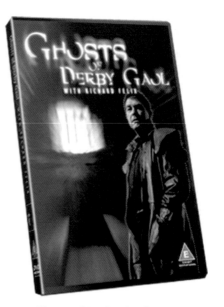

Ghosts of Derby Gaol DVD

Ghosts of Dudley Castle DVD

So you want to be a Ghost Hunter DVD

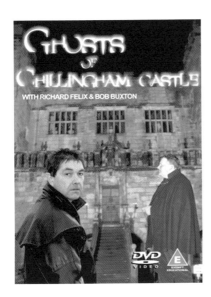

Ghosts of Chillingham Castle DVD

Ghosts of Annesley Hall DVD

 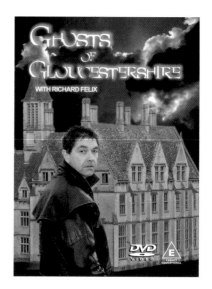

Ghosts of Essex DVD   Ghosts of Gloucestershire DVD

All DVDs and books are available direct from the producers,

Felix Films Ltd, Derbyshire.

Tel: 0845 88 22 782.

Email: info@felixfilms.net

Order online at: www.felixfilms.net

For information about Richard visit: www.richardfelix.co.uk

Derek Acorah

Liverpool's own world famous TV medium and author of many
books including, Psychic Adventures of Derek Acorah and Ghost
Hunting with Derek Acorah.

For more information visit www.derekacorah.org

Croxteth Hall DVD

A documentary history of Croxteth Hall and the Molyneux family (Lords of Sefton) - told through the life story of Raymond Lempereur, chef to Lord Sefton for 24 years, and his wife Elda.

Available from the shop at Croxteth Hall.

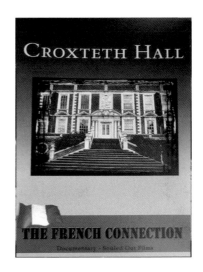

Para.Science

Para.Sceince was established to investigate, study and research into all types of paranormal phenomena. Investigations include extensive use of state - of - the - art equipment and is supported by a team of fully trained ASSAP accredited investigators.

All results of their investigations are made available to the public.

For more details visit www.parascience.org.uk

Tom Slemen

Author of many books of the Liverpool area including Haunted Wirral, Haunted Cheshire and Wicked Liverpool.

For more information visit www.tomslemen.tk